Supergrow

by Benjamin DeMott

NOVELS

The Body's Cage

A Married Man

ESSAYS

Hells & Benefits

You Don't Say

Supergrow

Supergrow

ESSAYS AND REPORTS ON

IMAGINATION IN AMERICA

BY Benjamin
DeMott

E. P. DUTTON & CO., INC.

NEW YORK   1969

Published simultaneously in Canada by Clarke, Irwin & Company
Limited, Toronto and Vancouver

Library of Congress Catalog Card Number: 71–82042

A 31975   [01]

NOTE: The essays in this book appeared originally (in some instances under
different titles or in different form) in *The American Scholar, Antioch Review, Book World, Educational Record, Esquire, New American Review,
The New York Times, Saturday Review,* and *The Urban Review.*

HOW TO RAISE A BRIGHTER CHILD (excerpt): © 1967 by Joan Beck. Reprinted by permission of Simon & Schuster, Inc.

GIVE YOUR CHILD A SUPERIOR MIND (excerpt): © 1966 by Siegfried and
Therese Engelmann. Reprinted by permission of Simon & Schuster, Inc.

Excerpt from poetry of Joel Oppenheimer: THE LOVE BIT. © 1962, Joel
Oppenheimer. Published by Corinth Books, New York.

Excerpt from UNDERSTANDING MEDIA by Marshall McLuhan: From UNDERSTANDING MEDIA by Marshall McLuhan. © 1964 by Marshall McLuhan.
Used with permission of McGraw-Hill Book Company.

Excerpt from W. H. Auden's *Lullaby:* © 1940 and renewed 1968 by
W. H. Auden. Reprinted from COLLECTED SHORTER POEMS 1927–1957 by
W. H. Auden by permission of Random House, Inc.

Florida Road Workers by Langston Hughes: From THE PANTHER AND THE
LASH by Langston Hughes. © 1967 by Arna Bontemps and George
Houston Bass. Reprinted by permission of Alfred A. Knopf, Inc.

Life Story by Tennessee Williams: Tennessee Williams, IN THE WINTER OF
CITIES. © 1956 by Tennessee Williams. Reprinted by permission of New
Directions Publishing Corporation.

Merritt Parkway by Denise Levertov: Denise Levertov, THE JACOB'S
LADDER. © 1958 by Denise Levertov Goodman. Reprinted by permission
of New Directions Publishing Corporation.

To Joey
Tom
Benj
&
Megan
Love from the old man—

Contents

Foreword

The essays collected in this book are about everything under the sun—rock music, improving your sex, the Hollywood life, the uses of poetry, Marshall McLuhan, violence in Mississippi, group-grope theater, student revolts at home and abroad. . . . And there isn't a unified tone and manner. Now the writer looks detached or even invisible; now he steps onstage and mugs a little; one minute he's in slippers in a study with fire and wine and cat (a relaxing ramble), and the next he's pressing an idea, selling something, obviously out to convince.

Still, there is one kind of unity: most of the pieces keep turning a single simple idea, namely, that people ought to use their imaginations more. For revolutionary sensibilities, this idea lacks charm. Using the imagination is felt to mean working for a sense of what it would be like to be Over There, on the other side, with the enemy. And revolutionaries consider that such work complicates passion, weakens the lust for confrontation, and leads as often as not to bargaining and other accredited mendacity. An example: The Black Panther Chairman abuses the black Supreme Court Justice (the latter having just denied a Cleaver plea) as an "Uncle Tom, a bootlicker, a nigger pig, a Tonto, and a punk." And at that moment I decide to undertake to "use my imagination." Why bother? asks the revolutionary. What will come of it, except some brooding to no purpose on intricacies and counter-pressures within the Supreme Court Justice's feelings? Why smooth out jaggedness and fury? Why fuzz up issues? We've been "imagining the other side of the question" for generations in this country: Why hang ourselves up, forever pondering the "true nature" of our Hitlers, Wallaces, Daleys, and the rest?

My belief is that this line is mistaken: the country hasn't arrived where it is because it's overpopulated with orgiasts of the personal imagination. Its problems are traceable largely to obliviousness, habitual refusal to harry private imaginations into constructing the innerness of other lives—both the life of the Supreme Court Justice and that of the Panther Chairman. Long ago, William James remarked that Americans refuse to see that foreigners "have insides of their own." This blindness has had clear consequences for recent American foreign policy, and if it were replaced with a measure of imaginative flexibility, it's doubtful that the sequel would be nothing but political blur. The claim of this book isn't, in short, that the reason for more reliance on the resources of the constructive imagination is that radical energies need dissipating; it is that the right use of the constructive imagination increases the effectiveness of those energies, enables people to anticipate moves and countermoves, prevents them from becoming frozen into postures of intransigence or martyrdom which, though possessing a "terrible beauty," have as their main consequence the stiffening of resistance and the slowing of change.

Two more words. The idea of imagining-from-within has vitality in numberless contexts unmentioned here. Nothing in these pages, for instance, about phenomenology or Husserl—and what post-Hegelian wouldn't chuckle at the picture of somebody running on about the personal idea, or being-for-itself, or the *Umwelt*, without touching that body of thought? Nothing here either about the psychological or developmental ramifications of the themes, and they are fascinating in themselves, as a hundred passages in Piaget attest:

> In verbal intercourse it would seem that children do not understand each other any better than they understand us. The same phenomenon occurs between them as between them and us: the words spoken are not thought of from the point of view of the person

spoken to, and the latter, instead of taking them at their face value, selects them according to his own interest, and distorts them in favor of previously formed conceptions. . . . This phenomenon occurs, it is true, among adults. But these have had at least some practice in argument or conversation, and they know their faults. They make an effort to understand and be understood, unless indeed distrust or anger reduces them to a childish state, because experience has shown them the appalling density of the human mind. Children have no suspicion of this. They think that they both understand and are understood.

[Language and Thought of the Child]

—But the subject launched is, after all, endless, and these collected glances around the culture scene weren't in my mind means of situating a theme solidly in a system of thought or inquiry: they were simply chances to bring an old idea into sight again and put some claims for it in passing.

Finally, there's the matter of how to judge my implied argument or cause as a whole—and I admit I'm defensive about this. Is the fair test, for someone who's on about the marvels of the imagination, how well he uses his own? Do we say: Has this writer earned the right to puff the imagination in general by showing that his own in particular is swell? Now and then I act as though I believed that test were fair—but it is an act. My failures or successes at seeing what was going on in the mind, say, of an adversary teacher in Mississippi or in the minds of a homosexual's neighbors at an eastern watering place—these determine the "quality of a piece," but little more than that. The case is that the arena in which to judge the worth of the sort of imagining most often spoken of in this book isn't literary (Jack is a better writer than Jim, etc.). The testing arena is dailiness, ordinary human encounter, family life experience, the supper table. And about the value of the imagination on that turf there really isn't any arguing: take the stuff away, and none of us, tads or dads, can live.

AMHERST, MASSACHUSETTS
January 9, 1969

Supergrow

"But He's a Homosexual...."

What is a homosexual artist? A devil and a liar, says the current noisy indictment—a desecrater, a self-server, a character nobody on earth should trust. Sly and sulky, he poisons hope and idealism with the mean flow of his resentment. Sick and exhibitionistic, he jams the media with neuroses, teaching that Women are destroyers and heterosexual domestic life is hell. Worse by far, the man is power-mad. Skinnying his way onto established grant committees, prize panels, editorial boards, and other seats of authority, he spurns aspirants not of his clique, thereby creating a tyranny of taste that soon will have every center of imaginative expression—theater, opera, symphony hall, publishing house, museum, gallery—under its cheesy thrall. In sum: The homosexual artist is an enemy of the people, a threat to the quality of American life.

As every magazine reader knows, indictments like the foregoing have for some time been highly salable. For a representative sample, consider an article about Messrs. Albee, Warhol, et al.—the title was "Who's Afraid of Aunt Fanny?"—that appeared a while back in *Ramparts*. The initial stance of this piece was one of tolerant sophistication; the author, Gene Marine, gave assurances that he was no scandalmonger, no keyhole inquirer into celebrities' private lives, no naïf eager to set up equations between, say, "long-haired hippies" and homosexuality:

> Let me put things straight [he wrote], for you and the libel lawyers. I don't absolutely know for certain the names of any famous homo-

sexuals, though I probably make the same guesses you do, and if I did know any for certain, I wouldn't tell you. As far as I know, Edward Albee is a square family man, Andy Warhol is afflicted with satyriasis and California has no homosexuality south of the Santa Ynez river. I couldn't care less.

But having given these assurances, Marine went on to prove them spurious. Employing the tricks of an innuendo-cutie and a manner of sleazy downrightness, he developed an ever more expansive series of charges, and ended by dealing damnation round the entire American cultural landscape. Here are some steps in the progress:

> The point is that homosexual playwrights and homosexual directors and homosexual producers are having more and more to say about what can and can't be done in an American theater.

> People who know more about it than I do . . . tell me that it's even worse in the world of art—by which I mean painting and sculpture. The galleries take what the decorators want them to take, and the decorators want them to take their gay friends.

> I'm getting damned tired of all the art being campy and all the plays being queer and all the clothes being West Fourth Street and the whole bit. *Some* I don't mind, but it's getting too close to *all*, and I have the feeling that there are healthier bases for a culture.

> You can take almost any part of the world of culture, and there it is, in bold lavender. Dance and interior design, fashions (women's *and* men's), music—especially outside the relatively virile jazz and rock fields—and music promotion, novels and poetry, little theater and magazines.

The ploy in question is, predictably, more or less standard throughout the contemporary muckraking press. (*Fact* enlarged the area of presumed "domination" by printing a "study" of homosexuals in TV.) And hints of the influence of this ploy— more about them in a minute—have been visible in journals of a quite different character: the Sunday drama section of *The New York Times*, highbrow periodicals like the *New York Review of Books* and the *Drama Review*.

That the subject of homosexual influence in the arts should engage attention at this moment isn't mysterious. American interest in matters cultural and aesthetic is on the rise. New levels of candor about sexual behavior seem to be achieved every other week. And, most important, the national reserves of credulity have not diminished much over the years. If this were not so, baiters of homosexual art probably would pull smaller audiences. For their charges are rooted in the belief that centralized control of the arts can be achieved by a nonpolitical, essentially nonideological nonorganization—and only the credulous can rest comfortably in such faith. Tyrannies of taste do occur, to be sure—they are inevitable whenever a professionally practiced art lacks multiple centers of power. (Serious music is the sector of the arts that most nearly meets the latter description at this moment. Outlets for the work of living American composers are extremely few, which means that homosexual cliquishness could—some informed people say it does—throttle free musical expression.) And homosexual centers of power do exist—a cluster of art galleries here, a group of experimental moviemakers there. (One famous Fifty-seventh Street gallery has even been, in fairly recent days, a center of homosexual poetry as well as of painting and sculpture.)

But countless other galleries flourish that are nothing of the sort, and a half-dozen low-budget cinematic experimenters continue to produce—and exhibit—films untouched by what is called "homosexual fantasy." And in other sectors of the arts mixed situations seem generally the rule. The financial backers of one newly founded off-Broadway production firm are homosexuals; those of several other newish producing firms are not. A few trade publishing houses appear to be particularly well disposed to homosexual writers; the majority have no clear policy save the pursuit of profit. Given present complications and uncertainties of taste and prejudice, and given the continued emergence from time to time of new centers of activity (the American Place Theatre is an example), the danger of total domination will remain slight. Cliquishness cannot be abolished, and, as just indicated, it can cause damage in fields of artistic endeavor where opportunities for professional hearing are subject to autocratic control. But, while complacency about these fields is inexcusable, they are less numerous then scourgers of "homosexual tyranny"—and the more gullible of their readers—profess to believe. And the heralded culture explosion should reduce their number, not increase it, in the future.

But if the homosexual himself isn't a serious threat to cultural vigor and variety, the same can't be said of those who harass him in print. The point at issue here isn't, true enough, easy to grasp. A piece writer who beats up "the fairies" for a few thousand words would seem, on the face of it, only another harmless canny profiteer. It's plain, after all, that complaints about "homosexual art" will never mobilize hostility and frustration at the destructive levels sustained in yesteryear by the Red-baiters.* And conceivably "frank talk" in this area, no matter how woolly and superstitious, can have beneficial effects. (The public needs to be reminded, some say, that reputations in the arts are made things, not miracles: edifices built by the continuous effort not simply of a single artist but of friends who sometimes praise a man's work when what they actually value is his personal charm. And the public needs the experience, others say, of *talking* about homosexuality—because such talk fosters the growth of tolerance: when homosexuality in one quarter of the community is freely and openly assessed, responses to homosexuality in the community at large should become less hysterical.) Why turn hypercritical toward characters who, whatever their own personal cynicism, may function as nourishers of American sophistication?

The answer is simple: At the center of most talk about "homosexual art" lies the assumption that books, pictures, poems created by homosexuals are private documents, narrow in range,

---

* Two mythy items that figure in "thinking" about the coming homosexualization of America are the concept of a nation asleep at the switch, as it were, too absorbed in business to notice its sex is changing, and the concept of a doomsday recognition scene, a moment at which people discover to their horror that they have frittered away their birthrate and are the last generation of their kind. Both concepts figured, in slightly different form, in Senator McCarthy's speeches on the Commie conspiracy a decade ago.

incapable of speaking truly to anyone not himself a homosexual. The prime effect of this already widely disseminated idea has been to neutralize or denature several of the most provocative critical images of contemporary life to win mass audiences since World War II. And from this it follows that the self-appointed enemy of "homosexual art" isn't just a nuisance: he is a pernicious waster of an invaluable cultural resource.

As might be guessed, the ways of waste—the means by which commentators cheat the work of homosexuals and torture it out of strength—are nothing if not ingenious. Chief among them is a trick of medical inside-dopesterism that transforms texts clear enough on their surface into complex codes or allegories—productions whose deepest truths yield themselves only to psychoanalytic exegesis. Consider, for instance, the operations of clinical exegetes on Edward Albee's *Who's Afraid of Virginia Woolf?* In both the stage and film versions, the ending of this work seems a moment of poignance. Weary beyond fury, blasted (almost) into kindness, George and Martha have arrived at a nowhere world in which combat is pointless. The audience knows that cozy murmurs about reconciliation, forgiveness, happiness ahead would be puerile, but is nevertheless aware of a passage into an atmosphere of feeling less ridden by fantasy, more open, more yielding. Nobody has "won," but a loss has been suffered jointly: pity is in the room.

Enter the clinical exegete, and every "simplistic" reading of the play is laved in scorn. (Exegetes of this brand are printed in psychoanalytic journals as well as in magazines of art.) *Virginia Woolf*, wrote Dr. Donald M. Kaplan (a psychoanalyst) in the *Drama Review*, is in its essence a predictable homosexual claim that "genitality is . . . an unnecessary burden"; the closing scene is a moment of triumph, it signifies that a married man "can prevail through the tactics of pregenital perversity" and need not grow up to his role:

> The sexuality of the parental bedroom [Nick and Martha offstage] is no match for the multifarious derivatives of George's oral aggression, anality, voyeurism, masochism and procreative reluctance. In

the end, Martha returns to George, as she so often has in the past. The enfant terrible again triumphs over the cocksmen of the outside world, and the nursery is preserved. . . .

Fitted into this pattern of homosexual aggression and glee, Albee's play is easily dismissed as a projection of dementia—a set of remarks about Rorschach cards, a collection of symptoms, nothing a "straight" could even begin to take straight.

Clinical exegesis isn't, of course, the harshest line of critique found in discussion of so-called homosexual art. Traditional American manliness makes itself heard in *Fact* and *Ramparts* ("I *like* women," Gene Marine said stoutly) and even in tonier periodicals—witness Philip Roth's attack on Albee's "pansy prose" that appeared in the *New York Review* following the opening of *Tiny Alice*. But the survival of tough-guyism is less interesting—and less regrettable—than the nearly universal acceptance of the central assumption just mentioned, namely, that art produced by homosexuals is irrelevant to life as lived by nonhomosexuals. A year or two ago the Sunday theater section of *The New York Times* printed a pair of articles by Stanley Kauffmann, then the newspaper's drama critic, on the "subject of the homosexual dramatist." A liberal, humane man, Kauffmann clearly had no terror of "perverts," no desire to suppress the work of the artists he was discussing. His articles, seen by many as another heroic breakthrough for frankness, dealt in passing with the matter of "homosexual style," and with the supposed tendency of the homosexual writer to treat theme and subject as immaterial and surface as all-important. They were partly conceived as defenses of the homosexual's right to freedom of expression, and they offered several telling observations about uses and abuses of that right.

Yet everywhere in his comments this critic signified his conviction that plays by homosexual dramatists should be regarded as codes to be deciphered, disguises to be seen through, private languages requiring continuous acts of translation by the audience:

In society the homosexual's life must be discreetly concealed. If he is to write of his experience, he must invent a two-sex version of the one-sex experience that he really has.

Kauffmann blamed this situation upon society—not upon the homosexual writer. And he argued forcibly for an end to the repression and inhibition that harries these writers into deceit:

If we object to the distortion that homosexual disguises entail, and if, as civilized people, we do not want to gag these artists, then there seems only one conclusion. The conditions that force the dissembling must change.

But, like the psychoanalyst quoted earlier, Kauffmann was committed to the notion that a homosexual's image of life is necessarily an expression of "homosexual truth"; the man has no choice except to "transform [what he knows] to a life he does not know, to the detriment of his truth and ours."

Even those critics whose avowed purpose is to make a case *for* "homosexual art"—as it is—to rescue it from vulgar attack and place it in a dignified light—fall into modes of discourse that are reductive and evasive in discussing its meaning. Consider the approach adopted in Susan Sontag's "Notes on Camp." This critic announces herself to be "strongly drawn" to the kind of art she is setting out to describe; yet throughout her essay she speaks of that art always as a phenomenon of style alone; the worth of its statement, the nature of its view of life, even its cultural associations and origins are passed off as boring matters. ("One feels," says the critic, "if homosexuals hadn't more or less invented Camp, some one else would.") What counts about this art is its *tonality,* not the total experience offered and the meanings created through that experience:

Camp and tragedy are antitheses. There is seriousness in Camp (seriousness in the degree of the artist's involvement), and, very often, pathos. The excruciating is also one of the tonalities of Camp; it is the quality of excruciation in much of Henry James . . . that is responsible for the large element of Camp in his writings. But there is never, never tragedy.

The obvious question is: Given the nature of the life represented in a so-called "Camp novel," is the quality of excruciation tendentious or appropriate? Can a man learn or confirm any truth of experience through a confrontation with Camp? When such questions aren't asked, much less answered, the implication is that this art may truly be empty of substance.

The point at stake bears restating. Dumb-ox or tough-guy or Philistine versions of works of art produced by homosexuals tend to be crudely dismissive—too crudely dismissive, often, for educated audiences to accept. But other dismissive lines have now become available. There is chic psychoanalytical chatter that evades the truth of a scene by seeing the scene as a symptom. There is a liberal critique that evades the truth of a scene by tolerantly viewing the scene, not as an image of life, but as a product of indirect censorship. And there is a brand of aesthetic criticism that evades the truth of a scene by focusing solely on matters of form. None of the approaches mentioned appears hostile to the so-called homosexual artist; each embodies different values and assumptions. But all are alike in espousing, or else in refusing to challenge, the dogma that the homosexual's representation of life can be only an expression of homosexual truth—"his truth" as opposed to "ours," as Kauffmann put it. And that dogma, while comforting to the majority, is quite without foundation.

It is probable that most readers and theatergoers—save for the scandalmongers who shriek about homosexual tyranny—will accept the claim that the most intense accounts of domestic life and problems in recent years, as well as the few unembarrassedly passionate love poems, have been the work of writers who are not heterosexual. The problem of compulsive promiscuity, or Don Juanism—one that Jose Ortega y Gasset described as the most delicate and abstruse in contemporary human relations—has been examined with extraordinary force and directness by

Tennessee Williams in several plays. And that intensity has time and time over proved to be an illumination of a kind. Some of the writers in question can be overpraised, to be sure. There is phony elegance and needless obfuscation in Albee's current manner, total dishevelment in the bulk of Ginsberg, too much self-indulgence in Williams, who seems bent on writing the same play four hundred times.

Yet a fair assessment of these writers, or of any of their relevant superiors—Genêt and Auden for two—can hardly be wholly negative. With a few other poets and dramatists, they are the only compelling writers of the postwar period who seem to know anything beyond the level of cliché about human connectedness, whose minds break through the stereotypes of existential violence or Nietzschean extravagance into recognizable truths and intricacies of contemporary feeling. They are not purveyors of situation comedy or Bond banalities or *Playboy* virility or musical-marital bliss (*I Do! I Do!*) or mate-murders. A steady consciousness of a dark side of love that is neither homo- nor hetero-sexual but simply human pervades much of their work; they are in touch with facts of feeling that most men do not or cannot admit to thought. They know what Catullus knew about *odi et amo*—simultaneities of hatred and its opposite—and they know the special terms and strains of these simultaneities in modern experience, wherein prohibitions against self-indulgence have lost force. They know that love and suffering are near allied and that love ought not to be confused with the slumbrous affection or habitual exploitation that is the rule in numberless households. They know that the lover's demand for exclusive possession has vanity as one of its roots.

They have in mind, not as aphorisms but as potential behavior and gesture, knowledge of the kind compressed in Mme. de Staël's remark that love equals self-love *à deux*, or in Proust's claim that there are people for whom there is no such thing as reciprocated love, and that these people are by no means the most insensitive among us. They know that instability is a fact of love, as of human personality generally. And the tensions and furies arising from contradictory desires and impulses seem to them proper subjects for intelligence to probe.

As good an exhibit as any, perhaps, is Auden's much celebrated "Lullaby":

Lay your sleeping head, my love,
Human on my faithless arm;
Time and fevers burn away
Individual beauty from
Thoughtful children, and the grave
Proves the child ephemeral:
But in my arms till break of day
Let the living creature lie,
Mortal, guilty, but to me
The entirely beautiful.

Soul and body have no bounds:
To lovers as they lie upon
Her tolerant enchanted slope
In their ordinary swoon,
Grave the vision Venus sends
Of supernatural sympathy,
Universal love and hope;
While an abstract insight wakes
Among the glaciers and the rocks
The hermit's sensual ecstasy.

Certainty, fidelity
On the stroke of midnight pass
Like vibrations of a bell,
And fashionable madmen raise
Their pedantic boring cry:
Every farthing of the cost,
All the dreaded cards foretell,
Shall be paid, but from this night
Not a whisper, not a thought,
Not a kiss nor look be lost.

Beauty, midnight, vision dies.
Let the winds of dawn that blow

Softly round your dreamng head
Such a day of sweetness show
Eye and knockng heart may bless,
Find the mortal world enough;
Noons of dryness see you fed
By the involuntary powers,
Nights of insult let you pass
Watched by every human love.

Reductions of this poem to homily or "general truth" play into the hands of Auden's detractors—those given to abusing the poet for being overchic. But that risk can be run. Some of the distinction of the "Lullaby" lies in the steadiness of its refusal to exclude the narrative consciousness from the lyric consciousness; joy, love, enchantment are placed, in this poem as in life, in immediate, living, indismissible adjacency to their opposites. Another part of the poem's distinction lies in the capacity of the singer at once to inhabit the lullaby-trance of union, to experience it in its fullness and uniqueness, and to look on from outside, acknowledging, neither merely pityingly nor merely knowingly, the replicability (in an age of indulgence) of this "ordinary swoon." And everywhere in the poem there is an alertness to contrarieties and puzzles of response—the murderously brief and beautiful sense of moral being perfected in sensual delight.

> Grave the vision Venus sends
> Of supernatural sympathy,
> Universal love and hope . . .

In this small poem a densely instructive world of feeling is created, a world that is proof against the simplicities of desiccation (the typist in *The Waste Land*), as well as against those of romantic melancholy (Frederick Henry in *A Farewell to Arms*). And in Auden's *Collected Poems* there are a number of songs— see for instance the matchless lyric "Warm are the still and lucky miles"—worth equal praise.

Does the knowledge embodied in such poems qualify as unique? Is it in itself a guarantee of "profundity"? Of course not:

most reflective men know what these poems know—namely, that
love is the only human entrance into an ideal world, and that life,
a teaser and mocker, lets few men through to stay. Why then is
such knowledge more vivid in homosexual art than elsewhere?
Again quick answers are unsatisfactory. Heroicizing the "homosexual artist" is, certainly, as senseless as condescending to him as
a case. It does need to be said, though, that the homosexual
artist's aptitude for the presentation of certain human (not
homosexual or heterosexual) complications of feeling can't be
understood by people oblivious to the features of his situation
that lend it a measure of dignity. "To be free is to have one's
freedom perpetually on trial." It isn't necessary to endorse every
line of existential scripture to see the application of this text from
Sartre to the intelligent, responsive homosexual who has a gift for
the formed re-creation of experience. The latter gift is, as everyone knows, distributed according to no visible plan; sexuality
conceived as a pure and separable essence is not its determinant.
But the homosexual who possesses it does have special occasion
to exercise and refine it in fundamental, as well as in craft or
professional, areas of life, owing to the peculiarities of his situation in the general culture. If I am a Citizen, Husband, Straight-
Arrow, I easily can put myself on trial. I can speak for a troubling
cause, enter upon a bout of promiscuity, teach in a turtleneck,
grow my hair long in back. But I cannot escape the promise of
ease, the possibility of subsiding into the accepted and the
respectable; always an oasis of habitual, unexamined, unjudged
life awaits me.

The intelligent homosexual, however, is in another situation. A
tide of suspicion flows toward him, perpetually demanding that
he justify his difference; relaxation into unthinking self-acceptance in the presence of other eyes is prohibited. If he is rich and
shrewd, he may manage to create for himself the illusion of a life
unexposed to antipathetic scrutiny—but sustaining that illusion is
hard work. If he isn't rich and shrewd, his immediate confronta-
tions with hostility—the interruptions of his taken-for-granted
daily existence—will be numberless. And these interruptions will

induce in him a heightened awareness of the feelings and assumptions of others—an immediate living consciousness of the
fragility of the shields that hide human cruelty from general
view.

To say this isn't for a moment to suggest that lives can, by any
system of categorization, be precisely compared in terms of their
remoteness from challenge: we measure with inklings and intui-
tions here, and confidence isn't in the equation. Neither is it to
suggest that the intelligent and sensitive homosexual is the only
man who is ever thrust into tasking encounters with himself and
others. It is to say that these encounters are probably more
difficult for the homosexual to avoid than for other men. And the
encounters do have "excruciating" value to anyone whose art
depends finally upon his ability to experience dailiness rather
than simply pass through it, to inhabit moment-to-moment reality, to be aware of present time and know it not as something
between yesterday and tomorrow but as the edge of his life.
Admittedly a man of strong mind can close himself off from the
coarseness that teases the homosexual in his round of errands in
any town or suburb other than a gay colony—schoolchildren
mincing behind his back as their elders have more or less in-
structed them to do, overheartiness or dropped eyes among
tradesmen, slyness and lubricity in the cleaning woman. And the
danger of sentimentalizing experience of this kind, assigning
more value and meaning to embarrassment than it possesses, is
real. Everyone knows about homosexual arrogance; everyone
knows that aristocratic poses fend off "nights of insult"; everyone
knows that flights of defensive scorn or resentment—the familiar
gestures of mediocrity—are common in homosexual conversation.

But self-deception and mediocrity are, after all, everywhere the
rule—and the writers and artists spoken of publicly as homosexuals, and thus looked down upon, are by and large not
mediocrities. They are men who have been *provoked* into dwelling on the relative emptiness and unthinkingness of most men's
commitments to the terms of their own lives. They are people
whom we put on endless trial, because our manner declares that

no condition of moral being except our own can be approved, because our explicit claim is that love can only be a permanent attachment, and because we dare not detach ourselves from our "institutions" even though we know they derive in great part from superstition. They are people forced to face up to the arbitrariness of cultural patterns—arbitrariness that we insist on regarding as altogether unarbitrary, a logical bidding of nature, a sane, wholly explicable pattern, like the movement of the earth. The fury that lifts James Baldwin's prose to eloquence, when that writer has before him the cruelty of cultural arbitrariness, stems not alone from Baldwin's experience as a Negro. And the racking power of those moments in Genêt, when this writer has the same spectacle in sight, arises not only from a career as thief. The usefulness of the instruction offered through this eloquence and power doesn't vary in accordance with the condition of the reader's sexuality. We need not be "perverts" to see into the life of that moment when Genêt's Divine enters the café, smiles round the room in "her" crazy aloneness, tests the blade of hate:

> She smiled all around, and each one answered only by turning away, but that was a way of answering. The whole café thought that the smile of (for the colonel: the invert; for the shopkeepers: the fairy; for the banker and the waiters: the fag; for the gigolos: "*that* one"; etc.) was despicable. Divine did not press the point. From a tiny black satin purse she took a few coins which she laid noiselessly on the marble table. The café disappeared, and Divine was metamorphosed into one of those monsters that are painted on walls—chimeras or griffins—for a customer, in spite of himself, murmured a magic word as he thought of her:
> "Homoseckshual." [*Our Lady of the Flowers*]

The making of a monster—a demon fabricated by simple habitual acts of *learned* disgust—is the theme momentarily in view here. And the reader who regards his imperviousness to it as a badge of moral distinction is at best a pious fool.

The case I am urging is, needless to say, open to a hundred misunderstandings. Someone says: You pretend that you aren't claiming that the homosexual is more sensitive to certain aspects of human relations than the heterosexual. But haven't you just been saying that homosexuals have insights that are denied to heterosexuals? Answer: Not quite. The notion of denial over-simplifies the issue, leaves out important parts of the full context. The difference between what the homosexual sees and what the heterosexual sees can't be explained in narrow physiological terms. Neither kind of sexuality can be separated from the culture and regarded as a physical or neurological thing-in-itself determining degrees of insight. Homosexuality, like heterosexual-ity, is a situation, a complex set of relations between self and society: the nature of these relations determines to some extent the special quality of the perceptions that each perceptive man can have. The relations vary with time and place; surely there are few significant likenesses between the situations of homosexuals in the arts in New York City now and the situations of their counterparts in, say, Paris in 1815 or London in 1600. There isn't, in short, any abstract entity properly called "homosexual insight" or "heterosexual insight"; there are only differences in the kinds of life situations in which intelligence tests itself. And these are the differences that shape the artist's vision.

Again, another query: You seem almost to imply that someone reading a poem or play dealing directly with homosexual experi-ence could nevertheless achieve—through his encounter with this work of art—deeper understanding of aspects of strictly hetero-sexual relationships. Do you really mean this? Answer: Yes. Look for a minute at the poem by Tennessee Williams called "Life Story."

> After you've been to bed together for the first time,
> without the advantage or disadvantage of any prior
>   acquaintance,
> the other party very often says to you,
> Tell me about yourself, I want to know all about you,
> what's your story? And you think maybe they really
>   and truly do

sincerely want to know your life story, and so you light up
a cigarette and begin to tell it to them, the two of you
lying together in completely relaxed positions
like a pair of rag dolls a bored child dropped on a bed.

You tell them your story, or as much of your story
as time or a fair degree of prudence allows, and they say,
            Oh, oh, oh, oh, oh,
each time a little more faintly, until the oh
is just an audible breath, and then of course

there's some interruption. Slow room service comes up
with a bowl of melting ice cubes, or one of you rises to pee
and gaze at himself with mild astonishment in the bath-
      room mirror.
And then, the first thing you know, before you've had time
to pick up where you left off with your enthralling life story,
they're telling you *their* life story, exactly as they'd intended
      to all along,

and you're saying, Oh, oh, oh, oh, oh,
each time a little more faintly, the vowel at last becoming
no more than an audible sigh,
as the elevator, halfway down the corridor and a turn to
      the left,
draws one last, long, deep breath of exhaustion
and stops breathing forever. Then?

Well, one of you falls asleep
and the other one does likewise with a lighted cigarette in
      his mouth
and that's how people burn to death in hotel rooms.

Not a masterwork to be sure, much too easily and sardonically
knowing a poem, too pleased by its own blackishness, and
perhaps also too needlessly "daring" in its sequence of third-
person masculine pronouns. But "Life Story" is a sharp perception of relations between promiscuity and the self-regard and self-
absorption of an age gone mad for Identity—and the sense of

this relatedness is as much an illumination for the straight world as for the queer.

And one more hostile question: You ask for pity, understanding, admiration for homosexual artists—thus suggesting that these are badly mistreated people of this day. Are they? Aren't they in reality all the cry just now? If we put them under pressure, they, for their part, do find excellent means of freeing themselves. And, finally: Suppose it *is* granted that the best "homosexual art" is indeed art—art without modifier; are we obliged to be decent to the worst? When we go off for a night at the theater and encounter something amounting simply to a play in drag, must we smother resentment?

The answer is that of course homosexual artists, like other ones, can be inferior, and that of course these artists have invented ways of easing the pressure we put them under. They do on occasion compose fantasies. They do on occasion express *their* resentment. They do on occasion revenge themselves through sexual disguises in plays and poems. They mock our solemnities with Happenings and joke pictures and weirdo flicks. They parody the ceaseless commercial agitation of "straight" sexual appetites. They create an art heavily dependent (see Genêt) on magic and metamorphosis, an art usually thin in political content, relatively unconcerned with what are called "public issues." And they can give themselves over to glee at the thought that whatever we think of them, few among us match them in brio or brilliance.

But these satisfactions can scarcely outweigh all torments— and, in any event, the fact that an achievement has earned a reward usually is not thought of as ground for discounting the achievement. And there are achievements here—this is the point of moment. A portrait of a man exacerbated by a woman need not be only a thrust at a generalized Enemy; in at least one American play such a portrait faced a mass audience with truths about the new world of sexual equality and universal self-absorption quite inexpressible either in Ibsen or Bernard Shaw. An image of egos dependent upon a fantasy child can be more than a faggish leer: in one American play such an image showed mean uses of the family and, in addition, the vapidities of the doctrine that procreation in itself equals fulfillment. And, by the same token, artists with extensive experience of respectable marriage and child rearing may write with seeming authority about subjects the homosexual can "never know," and yet be worthless—because they are blind to the truth that the acceptable life, the embrace of heterosexuality, can become a cliché, an automatized rather than freely created value.

The canard that negation is not necessarily stupidity and affirmation not necessarily illumination does, in fine, need summoning once more—in discussion of "homosexual art." Nobody is obliged to accept Nietzsche's claim that "every good thing, even a good book which is against life, is a powerful stimulant to life." But the sort of mind that seeks to place all hostility to established institutions as proof of disease does dirt on the revolution of candor that we claim to prize. Failure to hear out the homosexual artist with a seriousness matching his own, overeagerness to dismiss him as ignorant or perverse, assurance that we know what we are—this behavior at a time when Don Juans by the thousand jam the week-night motels and divorce rates soar and children everywhere are flogged into meaningless ambition—this is worse than senseless. It is a mockery not only of art and of the suffering that art rises out of and seeks to comprehend: it is a mockery of our famous, preening new liberation as well.

Against McLuhan

A marvy year for Marshall McLuhan, take it all in all. Tom Wolfe compared him with Darwin, Freud, and Einstein; Susan Sontag said in public she thought he was swell. London saw him as an epoch maker and intellectual frontiersman (*Encounter* and the *Times Lit Supp*), and *The New Yorker* reviewed him rapt. What is more, Academe—after a period of sitting tall but silent on his bandwagon—began talking out loud about his work. (One example: a recent international convocation of savants at Southern Illinois University spent days discussing the "communications revolution" in open session—mainly in McLuhanian terms.) Success being what it is, wasps and carpers were doubtless waiting for the man a piece or two up the road. But no amount of carping could obscure the facts of his rise. Overnight the author of *Understanding Media* had emerged as Midcult's Mr. Big. And ahead of him lay a shot at mass adulation and the title of Everyman's Favorite Brain.

The secret of this ascent isn't instantly visible to casual reportorial eyes. Marshall McLuhan is no literary old pro blessed with a power base and a rich experience at name-making. An English professor for most of his working life (Wisconsin, Assumption, St. Louis), he moved on from teaching only quite recently to his present post as director of Toronto University's Center for Culture and Technology. And despite long years in the classroom, he has no credit reserves in the trade—no stretch of unheralded, scholarly labor of the kind fellow professionals

35

pant to puff. McLuhan avoided book writing until he was forty. His first work, *The Mechanical Bride* (1951), was an analysis of the sex-power–horsepower ploy by which two generations of ad men have sold us our annual car. (Not much there for the Modern Language Association.) And after the *Bride* appeared, the author resumed his silence as a bookman and maintained it for another full decade and more.

Nor can it be said—still on the mystery of the McLuhanian boom—that here is a case of a late-blooming stylist, somebody who had to turn fifty to turn a slick phrase. In terms of style, this flower has yet to bud. Marshall McLuhan's present reputation rests on two books—*The Gutenberg Galaxy* (1962) and *Understanding Media* (1964); both are sometimes stimulating, but neither is pretty prose. One problem is that of opacity (McLuhan's pages are dense with stoppers like "sense ratios," "interiorizations of alphabetic technology," and the like). Another is that the favored method of organization has a bit too much in common with that of an impresario squirrel. *The Gutenberg Galaxy* looks gathered, not written: a paste-up from a hundred histories of math, political theology, nationalism, and fur trading, and from a thousand "other authorities." (Walt Whitman and Walt Whitman Rostow, Cicero and Father Ong, de Chardin and de Beauvoir, Rabelais, Riesman, and Shakespeare, the Opies, Powys, and Poe—name your hero, he surely is here.) The man's work reads for pages at a stretch like a Marboro clearance ad:

> Clagett [author of *The Science of Mechanics in the Middle Ages*] presents the treatise of Nicholas of Oresme *On the Configurations of Qualities* in which Oresme says: "Every measurable thing except numbers is conceived in the manner of continuous quantity." This recalls us to the Greek world in which as Tobias D. Dantzig points out in his *Number: The Language of Science* (pp. 141–2): "The attempt to apply rational arithmetic to a problem in geometry resulted in the first crisis in the history of mathematics. . . ." Number is the dimension of tactility, as Ivins explained in *Art and Geometry* (p. 7) [etc.].

Furthermore, the two leading articles of this thinker's gospel can't be called easy to grasp. The first is a theory of culture which contends that communications media impose a wide range of assumptions "subliminally." (The form of the media, not the content, structures men's values, according to McLuhan; the form also determines the content of the senses and the very look of the world.) The second is an interpretation of history which claims that revolutionary transformations of media occur periodically through the ages, and that one such transformation is in progress right now. (A five-hundred-year-old "typographic and mechanical" era is ending and an "electric galaxy of events" has begun; the new "galaxy" offers experiences of simultaneity and heightened interdependence in which traditional values—privacy, independence, and so on—are engulfed.) Neither of these items is wholly lacking in interest, and McLuhan's historical chapters are often enlivened by canny, comprehensible remarks. But the key idea, to repeat—that of the centrality of *form* in the media as the determinant of social structure and individual minds—is to most men unfamiliar and abstract. An author who makes it into his dogma would ordinarily be ill-advised to brood overmuch about fame.

That Marshall McLuhan is now in position (if he chooses) to brood about nothing else owes a little to his skill with the magic of the modern. "Baby, it's what's happening" is a regularly sounded ground theme in his work. The basic language is video-mesh, circuits and data processing. Injunctions to *Think Modern!* appear on page after page. ("We still have our eyes fixed on the rearview mirror looking firmly and squarely at the job that is receding into the nineteenth-century past.") The right names—Cage, Camp, Bond, Van Der Beek, the whole of the switched-on mob—are fingered throughout like sacred medals. The Farthest-Out Art—electric landscapes, pop Happenings or whatever—is treated either as classic or already passé, and idols of the hour are probed intensely, like important neglected codes:

"The Beatles stare at us with eloquent messages of changed sensory modes for our whole population, and yet people merely think how whimsical, how bizarre, how grotesque. The Beatles are trying to tell us by the antienvironment they present just how we have changed and in what ways."

Old times and old-timers do turn up, as indicated—especially in *The Gutenberg Galaxy*. But even they swim into the reader's ken to a definite R-and-R beat. (Who was Christopher Marlowe? The man, says McLuhan, turning dead Kit hummingly on, who "set up a national P.A. system of blank verse." Who was Heidegger? A cat who "surfboards along on the electronic wave." What were the Middle Ages? *"The Late Show* for the Renaissance.")

Among other crowd-pleasing elements in the McLuhanian equation, the author's literary persona rates a word. At some moments this writer plays Inside Dopester (I called the Kennedy-Nixon election, he announces; I knew exactly why Jack would win). At others he's simply a Scrappy Little Professorial Guy. Enemies as various as George Bernard Shaw ("he lost his nerve") and General Sarnoff ("the voice of the current somnambulism") are worked over in his books; Lewis Mumford, Arnold Toynbee, and dozens more are patronized, and English profs ("literary brahmins") come off naturally as jerks. The author also does a turn as Kitsch Cynic, mocker of goodie-good types—and it is here that he shows his best stuff, speaking again and again with the clarity of last night's knowing cabby or this week's issue of *Time*. People who are easily shocked give him the laughing fits. ("The historian Daniel Boorstin was scandalized by the fact that celebrity in our information age was not due to a person's having done anything but simply to his being known for being well-known. Professor Parkinson is scandalized that the structure of human work now seems to be quite independent of any job to be done.") And he likes interrupting the argument to defend the innocent guilty and to lean on moralizing twerps:

So great was the audience participation in the quiz shows that the directors of the show were prosecuted as con men. Moreover, press and radio ad interests, bitter about the success of the new TV medium, were delighted to lacerate the flesh of their rivals. Of course, the riggers had been blithely unaware of the nature of their medium, and had given it the movie treatment of intense realism, instead of the softer mythic focus proper to TV. Charles Van Doren merely got clobbered as an innocent bystander, and the whole investigation elicited no insight into the nature or effects of the TV medium. Regrettably, it simply provided a field day for the earnest moralizers. A moral point of view too often serves as a substitute for understanding in technological matters.

A literary self that amounts to an amalgam of Bogie and Dr. Huer might not seem everybody's dish; but the thing obviously meets a felt need.*

And the same can be said about McLuhan's gamesmanly ploys as a historian. A specialist in unnoticed causes, this scholar never delves into a historical situation without emerging with "major factors" nobody quite hit on before. The handling in *Understanding Media* of the advent of philanthropy a century ago is typical of his cunning moves. Why did "even the hardiest of the rich dwindle into modest ways of timid service to mankind"? Because of the invention of the telegraph, McLuhan explains—and does not stop for questions. What is the key factor in the southern civil-rights struggle? The internal-combustion engine. ("The real integrator or leveler of white and Negro in the South was the private car and the truck, not the expression of moral points of view.") Why were the Jews murdered by the million? Because radio came before TV. ("Had TV come first there would have been no Hitler at all.") The talent in question isn't the kind treasured by trad historians, but it is what is called provocative and universally pleasing to wits.

In the end it won't do, though, to pretend that Marshall

---

* There are occasional bad breakdowns or inconsistencies in this public literary mask. McLuhan stands forth usually as a man quite unafflicted by any sense of inferiority. "I am in the position of Louis Pasteur," he tells his reader repeatedly. Yet the word "humility" comes not infrequently to his lips. For example: his address at Southern Illinois, which began with a summary of likenesses between Marshall McLuhan and Plato, ended with the assertion that "I really feel shatteringly humble." It was a sequel that left some alert listeners confused.

McLuhan's secret is a matter either of mere wit or mere newsi.
ness or mere literary self-creation. The truth is more complicated
—and more painful—than that. Grasping it means facing up to
the dozen different kinds of stratagem by which this author
empties facts and agonies from the world he thinks of as "Now."
Some of these stratagems depend on tricks of futuristic projection, displacements of present-day reality which treat desperate
hopes as facts. (Write that "the real integrator of the white and
Negro *was*," and you imply that the struggle has already been
won.) Other tricks include sudden weird tonal abstractions—see
the flip comment about TV and Hitler—deadenings of feeling
and sympathy that distance holocaust and shame. Still others con
the reader into a frankly theatrical view of experience, a vision
that insulates him from immediacies and shows forth all life as a
production or stunt. Taken singly, needless to say, none of the
stratagems would rank as original, amazing, or troubling; taken
in concert they have powerful and obnoxious effect. The complaint isn't that Professor McLuhan puts together a thoroughly
fantastic account of the situation of contemporary man; it is that
he sets himself up, speaking bluntly, as the constituted pardoner
of this age—a purveyor of perfect absolution for every genuine
kind of modern guilt.

Do I chide myself for trivial failings—my laxness as a parent,
my sins of permissiveness, my failure to exact respect from the
kids? Do I worry about rearing layabouts incapable of work or
thought?—Oh, but come *on*, says Marshall McLuhan, a benign,
forgiving face, the truth is your children are grand:

> Some people have estimated that the young person, the infant and
> the small child, growing up in our world today works harder than
> any child ever did in any previous human environment—only the
> work he has to perform is that of data processing. The small child
> in twentieth-century America does more data processing—more work
> —than any child in any previous culture in the history of the world.
> . . . We haven't really cottoned on to the fact that our children work
> furiously, processing data in an electrically structured world. . . .

Do I feel bad about my *own* laziness, say—my own unending belt of mindlessness in front of TV? Situation comedy, secret agents, mean mockeries of domestic life . . . Has my intellectual appetite gone dead? My mind turned slush?—Forget it, says this Constant Comforter. The medium is the message, and whatever you think you are doing in front of the box, the fact is you're being expanded-extended-improved. "TV has opened the doors of audile-tactile perception to the nonvisual world of spoken languages and food and the plastic arts. . . ." TV has transformed "American innocence into depth sophistication, independently of 'content'. . . ." TV has "changed our sense-lives and our mental processes. It has created a taste for all experience in *depth*. . . . And oddly enough, with the demand for the depth, goes the demand for crash-programming [in education]. Not only deeper, but further, into all knowledge has become the normal popular demand since TV."

Or am I bugged by my pointless affluence, my guilt about having fat on my hide at a time when sores of starvation are the rule for hundreds of millions elsewhere?—But don't be *silly*, says my adviser; you're being ridiculous again. You're mired in outmoded thinking; you're the victim of moldy figs. Oh, yes, we've all heard about the underdeveloped nations, the "ascent into history," the necessity of hard labor, the problems of locating resources, building factories, educating work forces, creating credit systems, and the like. But *we* know, don't we now, *we* know that we have it within us practically at this instant to do the miracle of our choice whenever we choose:

> The computer will be in a position to carry out orchestrated programming for the sensory life of entire populations. It can be programmed in terms of their total needs, not just in terms of the messages they should be hearing, but in terms of the total experience as picked up and patterned by all the senses at once. For example, if you were to write an ideal sensory program for Indonesia or some area of the world that you wanted to leapfrog across a lot of old technology, this would be possible if you knew in the first place its present sensory thresholds, and, second, if you

had established what kind of sensory effect a given technology like radio or literacy had upon sensory life as a whole.

Or suppose I am simply worried about my *natural* self, my condition as part of the creation, my indecencies to the life around me that is coextensive with mine. I deface the garden, Earth, with cigarette butts, billboards, beer cans. I pollute the streams with uncycled wastes from my factory. Should I not then despise myself as a rapist?

Well, do what you like, answers Marshall McLuhan sniffishly, but you are a bit of a wag. Men may have been a bit hard on the planet in the past—but full amends are about to be made. If you'll just be patient a minute or two, you'll see us doing a kind of honor to this Little Old Earth that will more than make up for the past:

> If the planet itself has thus become the content of a new space created by its satellites, and its electronic extensions, if the planet has become the content and not the environment, then we can confidently expect to see the next few decades devoted to turning the planet into an art form. We will caress and shape and pattern every facet, every contour of this planet as if it were a work of art, just as surely as we put a new environment around it.

In sum: give it all over, is the message. Give over self-doubt, self-torment, self-hatred. Give over politics. Give over conscience. Relax, go soft and complacent, accept your subliminal perfectibility. Before us, almost at hand, is a moment of revelation when it shall be shown that "we are living in a period richer" than that of Shakespeare, that our time is properly thought of as "the greatest of all human ages, whether in the arts or in the sciences." And while we are waiting, there are worthy acts to be done. We can cut ourselves off from our depressions. We can look beyond the trivia of daily life—beyond entanglements with wives and children and employers, beyond neighbors, bond issues, tax bills, and the rest. We can overcome the tired sense that there are urgent local and international issues, and learn to see the drop-

out, the teach-in, even the casualty himself as part of The Greater
Showbiz:

> . . . we now experience simultaneously the dropout and the teach-
> in. The two forms are correlative. They belong together. The teach-
> in represents an attempt to shift education from instruction to dis-
> covery, from brainwashing students to brainwashing instructors.
> It is a big dramatic reversal. Vietnam, as the content of the teach-in,
> is a very small, misleading Red Herring. It really has nothing to do
> with the teach-in as such any more than with the dropout. The
> dropout represents a rejection of nineteenth-century technology as
> manifested in our educational establishments. The teach-in repre-
> sents a creative effort to switch the educational process to discovery,
> from package to prove.

Thus will we rise to the certainty that Style and Method are all,
that the visible—Vietnam or wherever—is not in any real sense
there. And having done this, we can take off absolutely, fly up
from the nonworld of consciousness into the broad sanctuaries of
ecstasy and hope. ("The computer, in short, promises by technology a Pentecostal condition of universal understanding and
unity . . . a perpetuity of collective harmony and peace.")

It is here, of course, precisely here—in the gift of oblivion—
that the heart of the McLuhanian munificence is found. This
writer does bestow on his reader a welcome grant of hip moder-
nity. He stimulates in addition a voluptuous sense of mastery (to
say "The Middle Ages were *The Late Show* for the Renaissance"
is rather like cornering a Corvette). And whether or not the basis
of his sunniness is sheer terror, his work does rank as the
strongest incitement to optimism yet produced in this age. But
the great gift offered is, ultimately, the release from consciousness
itself. Those who accept it have clearly won a deliverance, a free
way up and out.

Are they so reprehensible? it is asked. Poor men, the ignorant,
the hopeless, have to buy *their* release from pushers. The Professor's enthusiasts spend less and get more. They buy a guarantee that the disorder, chaos, and misery around them are but

veils and shadows, lies told by the stupid conscious mind—yet they make no sacrifice whatever of their ability to function in the workaday world. In the act of discounting their own senses and anxieties, they rise up to form an elite—men dignified by their access to the knowledge that nobody knows what's what. If they are at bottom blind devotees of the subliminal dogma, they have at least kept their self-respect.

—And in any case what *is* the compulsion to Gloomsville that makes it shameful to smile with a Happy Prof? By what laws are we obliged to speak and act always as though tragedy, endless tragedy, were the perpetual human lot? Is it really a badge of reason to hold at every hour of day and night that—as Santayana claimed—"the only true dignity of man is his capacity to despise himself"?

The frustration that breathes in these questions, the boredom with canting pessimism, the thirst for a freshening of life, the longing for an inward sense of courage—these are doubtless the deepest secrets known by our new King of Popthink, the deepest needs his elixir is designed to meet. And making light of the needs is no less inhuman than exploiting them. The best that can be done is to repeat the questions that consciousness—were there any of it left around—would probably feel bound to raise, viz.:

How much can be said for an intellectual vision whose effect is to encourage abdication from all responsibility of mind?

Or: What good is this famous McLuhanacy if it makes men drunk as it makes them bold?

Rock Saves?

All at once "they"—the opinion-makers, tastemakers, types who Know and Know—were hailing rock music as a high road to cultural and even spiritual salvation: should sane folk buy that jazz?

They're not likely to tomorrow, certainly. For most people pop music is one thing; intellectual or spiritual transformation is another; closing the gap between the two means rearranging a whole cluster of assumptions about art, order, and values. And while such rearrangements have occurred in the past, just at the moment some barriers exist. The most obvious barrier to grown-up, middle-class receptivity to rock is the disquieting life style of rock groups and audiences—the hair, the costumes, the volume, frightening hints of sexual liberation, etc. But there are others. One is the tendency of a number of preachers of rock as Revelation to shock rather than argue or explain—witness Allen Ginsberg's comparison of the Fugs with Jesus Christ: "The Bible says that when Christ comes back, 'every eye shall see.' . . . When the Fugs break thru . . . every eye shall see." Another is that rock lyrics are often, speaking gently, hard to fathom—witness the Lemon Pipers' "Jelly Jungle":

In the jelly jungle of orange marmalade
There are tangerine dreams waiting for you in orange marmalade
In the jelly jungle of orange marmalade.

Still another problem: rock seems at moments only a footnote to the pot or drug experience, not an independent meditative engagement in its own right. (William Kloman recently reported, in *The New York Times,* on the marked increase in rock records designed for use as background music for pot parties—"intricate harmonies, gently orchestrated melodies, and abrupt shifts in tempo which would strike the normal listener as pointless and distracting.")

And then beyond all this—a further obstacle to acceptance of rock as a vision—stands the seeming faddishness of the phenomenon. Lengthy picture and text rock stories in *Look* and *Life* and *Time,* rock commentary added to *The New Yorker's* regular cultural coverage, the commissioning, by the *New York Review of Books,* of essays on this or that rock group, the emergence of rock magazines like *Crawdaddy,* the density of rock pieces in pow periodicals along the spectrum from *Village Voice* to *Cheetah* to *Eye,* the rock interests of scenely figures like Marshall McLuhan, John Cage, and Susan Sontag, the apparent impossibility of contriving a radio or TV commercial without a rock beat—none of these can simply be laid at the door of a nasty music-biz flackdom. Yet together they encourage belief that rock is "merely" a fashion—part of the famous swinging Now-culture that is bound to age and may already be passing away. How can serious thought and feeling flourish amid such ephemerality?—so runs the inevitable squarish question.

That the idea of the new pop music as a religious force is so far credible only to With-Its doesn't signify, however, that it will never gain credibility for others. As already indicated, rock is now being taken seriously in many quarters usually thought to be proof against chichi or frivolity—the upper echelons of the United Presbyterian Church, for one. (The leadership of this institution recently retained a rock group called the Astrakhan Sleeve to produce religious records; a spokesman explained that rock is a "forum for serious messages far removed from the moon-June variety.") And there are signs that secular organs of opinion which, in the past, have exerted powerful, if trickle-down, influence on majority thought are moving in a comparable direction. On the appearance of the Beatles' last LP, *Partisan Review* carried a long tribute by Professor Richard Poirier, Chairman of English at Rutgers and a *PR* editor—an essay that invoked Shakespeare and T. S. Eliot in characterizing the Beatles' gifts, saw a likeness between their "knowledge" and that of contemporary writers like Beckett and Borges, and, at its climax, argued that the Beatles speak with an intensity of philosophical-aesthetic insight matched only by titans of the past:

> "And the time will come," it is promised in one of [the Beatles'] songs, "when you will see we're all one, and life flows on within you and without you." As an apprehension of artistic, and perhaps of any other kind of placement within living endeavor, this idea is allowable only to the very great.

And the Beatles are by no means the only group that has inspired writing at this pitch of awe. The third issue of *New American Review* carried a discussion of rock music by Professor Albert Goldman of Columbia in which a rock composition was compared to *King Lear,* and the group called The Doors was said to "achieve their purpose as gurus, which is to confront their audience with the most basic unbearable truths." In course of this essay Professor Goldman laid down numerous other claims for rock music:

> [Rock] has acted like a magnet, drawing into its field a host of heterogeneous materials that has fallen quickly into patterns. No other cultural force in modern times has possessed its power of synthesis.

> [Rock] has cleared a channel from the lowest and most archaic to the highest and most recent, and through that conduit is now flowing a revitalizing current of energy and of ideas. The result has been the elevation of rock to the summit of popular culture and the accelerating expansion of its interests and resources.

> By pushing toward higher levels of imaginative excellence, rock has begun to realize one of the most cherished dreams of mass culture; to cultivate from the vigorous but crude growth of the popular arts a new serious art that would combine the strength of native roots with the beauty flowering from the highest art.

Claims are just that, needless to say—claims. Some eyes confronting the ones just quoted may find vexing resemblances between them and youth cult paroxysms on the same subject—effusions like those of Mr. Gene Youngblood of the Los Angeles *Free Press:* "There is only one word for [Jimi] Hendrix: inspiring. He's an electric religion. . . . After he hurled his guitar at the screen in a cataclysmic-volcanic-orgasmic finale we fell back limp in our seats, stunned and numbed." But a resemblance of any sort between low-cult and high-cult accounts of the rock experience demands to be taken as evidence in itself that that experience is indeed no negligible "cultural force." The questions arising are: Why is rock making it, in the graceful phrase, so big? What specific qualities of this musical experience explain its attractiveness to rude youth, thoughtful youth, literary intellectuals, "cultivated minds"? Finally: Who among the mass of listeners can rock truly "save"—or truly harm—and how?

As may or may not go without saying, rock fans hold that the success of the movement is best understood in musical, not metaphysical, terms. And that argument isn't wholly absurd on its face. The movement has produced several inventions in the field of singing style (Ray Charles is the most gifted of the inventors). The performers in the "mainstream soul" division—in particular Aretha Franklin and the late Otis Redding—are not much inferior in freedom, exuberance, range of color, and individuality of phrasing to the best singers in jazz and blues history. A dozen Beatle songs can be played with delight by any amateur musician who relishes tunes with surprising changes, structural inventiveness, and melodic lines of uncommon length and sweetness. There are passages of genuine musical excitement—who is unaware of this?—throughout "Rubber Soul," "Revolver," and "The Magical Mystery Tour" (the entrance into "Blue Jay Way" is especially lovely). A fine fragment of music drama—the poised ironical stiff-arm called "Lady Jane"—turns up in a Rolling Stones album. (The Beatles best the stony Stones when the latter imitate them but not invariably otherwise; no third group can compete with either—even after so many years.) Several groups possess able instrumentalists (slightly overrated by rock fans)— the guitarists Mike Bloomfield and Eric Clapton, for two examples. And, viewed as a disaster epic, a Hendrix concert is only a shade less terrorizing—though there are no dancers and much less blackness—than the much-praised Merce Cunningham–La Monte Young "Winterbranch."

Moreover—still in the area of musical accomplishment—there are some feats of assimilation in the development of rock that have few parallels in the history of pop music. Over the past two decades, a long list of performers contributed directly and indirectly to the development in question. (Rock "began," in a sense, with a Cleveland disc jockey's decision, in 1954, to feature some obscure rhythm and blues records made by Negro record companies in the South.) Some names on the list are still familiar, either because the performers were superstars in their time or ours or because they remain active now—Elvis Presley, Chuck Berry, Ray Charles, the Everly Brothers, the Beatles, Bob Dylan. Others, who were in their way not less important, haven't quite become household words—Frankie Lymon, for instance, Bo Diddely, Little Richard, B. B. King, several more.

But the roster of names testifies that rock came to its eminence by mixing into the basic rhythm and blues texture other musical elements and traditions—materials that hitherto had had separate publics of their own. The audience for rhythm and blues records of the early fifties lay mainly in the black ghettoes of the North. But new vocal sounds that were added in the mid-fifties— the gospel sound (Little Richard), country and western (Presley), an unprecedented crossing of gospel and blues (Charles)— widened the audience geographically and socially. And there were comparable developments in instrumental sound and in rock lyrics. B. B. King, the guitarist, moved the rock band on from the scrappy haphazard sound of R & B, and other major contributions came from the eclectic Beatles, from the inventors of the supergorgeous Mantovanian Motown Sound, and from the pioneers of progressive or art rock. (As for rock lyrics: California surf and drag rock superimposed the "contented" experience of middle-class white youths upon the original blues-based shouts; Bob Dylan and the school of folk rock complicated the blend with political and social commentary; the works of the Stones and the Fugs steadily sharpened the ironical edge or fury of the commentary.) As Professor Goldman puts it:

> The Rock Age has assimilated everything in sight, commencing with the whole of American music: urban and country blues, gospel, hill-billy, Western "goodtime" (the ricky-tick of the twenties), and Tin Pan Alley. It has reached across the oceans for the sounds and rhythms of Africa, the Middle East and India. It has reached back in time for the baroque trumpet, the madrigal, and the Gregorian chant; and forward into the future for electronic music and the noise collages of *musique concrète.*

But while all this is true, the new musical possibility supposed to have been created by rock's assimilating power—the possibility of a "new serious art that would combine the strength of native roots with the beauty flowering from the highest art"—still looks frail and remote.* Market pressures touch rock no less directly than they have touched every other kind of music in the American pop past. As there were crashing mindless set pieces in the Swing Era to excite the go-go-go Saints! Saints! big-tipper mob ("One O'clock Jump," Sing Sing Sing"), so there are a hundred versions of Jimi Hendrix's "Wild Thing" and "Purple Haze" now (wilder and louder, naturally, than in Olden Times). As the dance bands of the late thirties "advanced" toward fancy charts, with cathedral voicings of reed sections (Glenn Miller) and few opportunities for individual musical creativity, so the

---

* Some jazz lovers claim that, for aesthetic reasons, it will ever be thus. But several rock groups—Cream, The Jefferson Airplane—have lately taken tentative steps toward meeting the flatly dismissive objections of the jazz buff. (The objections are that the high volume and blocky pounding monotonous 4/4 beat rule out rhythmic intricacy and pliancy, as well as subtlety in dynamics, and that, while there is a jazz and blues foundation to the music, improvisation has never become a prime feature of the form.)

famous Motown rock rises to a comparable glossiness at a comparable musical cost and commercial profit.

Again and again, in truth, the listener to rock records is haunted by echoes of the kitsch sounds of the thirties—not to mention echoes of the old anxieties about integrity vs. sellout. Martha and the Vandellas singing "My Baby Loves Me"—the background here is pure Big Sky music, appropriate for Joel McCrea's Arizona or for a De Mille epic or even (at a pinch) for backing some footage of the Olivier-Oberon *Wuthering Heights*. Diana Ross, that wispy lead singer heard on The Supremes' "Stop in the Name of Love"—her timbre (or no-timbre) is straight out of "Oh Johnny"-ville, is it not? And where, oh, where, in schlock rock like Tommy James and the Shondells, is there even so much as a memory of the authentic gritty joyousness of Otis Redding singing:

> On a cold, rainy, windy night
> She shut all the doors
> She cut off all the lights
> She holds me and squeezes me tight
> She tells me Big O everything's all right . . .
> Come on now
> Bring my breakfast to the table
> When I go to work she know's I'm able
> Do my job, I come back in
> You oughta see my baby's face
>
> She just grins, grins, grins

The progressive or art rock school does, to be sure, continue to experiment, and newish groups like The Doors conceive unusual ambitions and are more venturesome in pattern and theme than most of their American competitors. And there are the Beatles and the Stones. The Beatles, though, are in full flight from rock to a kind of show music—and it must be said, furthermore, that their smoothie, nice-lad manner never much engaged lovers of mainstream soul. As for art rockers like Van Dyke Parks, they don't sell. And while The Doors do, their trade appears to depend, not upon musical freshness, but upon exploitation of the sexiness of the singer Jim Morrison. (On one recent occasion Mr. Morrison began a public performance by recounting his latest sexual adventure; it had taken place five minutes before curtain time.)

The point of this glance at economics is that the subject has important bearing on the matter of the nature of the rock triumph. If the rock world were conscious of the junk, kitsch, and exploitative sexuality that litters the present scene, if alertness to differences of musical quality in rock material were the rule, the argument that the success of rock is essentially musical would be less implausible. As it is, the suspicion lingers that the rock experience is as impure, by musical criteria, as most of the pop experiences that have preceded it.

The jazz intelligentsia of the thirties tended to embrace the entire jazz enterprise, avoiding musical discriminations, invoking few standards save the one that permitted chuckles at the Lombardo brothers or Horace Heidt, excluding little that called itself jazz, regardless of how pretentious and incompetent the stuff might be. And the rock intelligentsia of the present day behaves similarly. (Professor Goldman avoids musical assessments entirely. Professor Poirier speaks of the Rolling Stones, the Left Banke, and the Bee Gees as equals—all are "exceptionally good"; a counterpart statement in the nonrock world would find Al Hirt and Liberace to be as interesting as Miles Davis and Thelonious Monk.) Three decades ago such refusals of judgment signified that the experience of listening to jazz was less musical than political in nature—an occasion on which a longed-for relationship (one of solidarity) between self and underdog or underadvantaged could be achieved. Nowadays the refusals signify that the experience of listening to rock is less musical than—

Well, than what? What exactly is the rock audience hankering after? We are back, if not at the theme of rock as salvation, then at a restatement of the truth that the key to the success of rock music appears to lie elsewhere than in the music itself—perhaps in an adjustment or harmony between certain extramusical features of the rock experience and certain extramusical needs or desires characteristic of the rock audience. But the questions remain: What needs? What desires? What precise means of gratification?

The familiar moral line—rock thrives among the educated because modern man thinks the test of an education is how far it enables you to spit at gentility—offers a way into the problem. Throughout the postwar decades popular culture has repeatedly been used by teacher and student alike as a weapon in a war against "liberal," "humane," or "highbrow" values of the past. Publicity is better than craft for an artist, murder is a means of self-improvement for everybody, says the novelist (Norman Mailer)—and the Sayings are instantly enshrined by university professors as mighty challenges to the "trad." TV is life, books are death, says the pundit (Marshall McLuhan)—and is hailed by whole congresses of teachers for smashing the venial-lineal past. "The Mona Lisa is crap," says the pop singer (John Lennon)—and intellectual reviews snap him salutes.

And the salutes aren't mysterious. Some are traceable, no doubt, to the self-contempt and desperate fantasy of academic men who, unnerved by the library life, mock those who are nourished by it, and dream of a golden world of organic illiterate pimps and pugs. Others, though, bespeak a determination to call the bluff of the older culture; they attest people's belief that the older culture has been "found out." Keep your voice down, don't bother the people next door, said that culture, counseling self-restraint, moderation, and sequential reasoning (as opposed to harrowing shrieks and groans). But when the people next door turned out to be Dachau people, Hiroshima people, Johannesburg and Selma people, the counsel was known at once to stink. What better counsel was available? Any advice, any sound free of complicity, had a superior claim. Any assertion that outraged the Establishment. For it was the governors, not the guitarists, who did the killing, while solid citizens looked impassively on. From which it followed, did it not, that virtue lies precisely in that which the governors find vile?

One use of rock, in short, was to *occasion* scorn—to stimulate the hypocrite to display his nature. Turn it down! Good Folk cry, in love with their own complacency. And that gesture against "being disturbed" reenacts (some say) a hundred hideous obliviousnesses of the past.

But there are other uses, for—peace to the moralist—rock fans don't wholly exempt themselves from sin. Their chief need, in fact (no sense, incidentally, pretending that only rock types share this need), their chief need is relief from significant life quandaries and guilt. And first among the quandaries is one that comes down roughly to this: I, an educated man (or adolescent), thoughtful, concerned, liberal, informed, have a fair and rational grasp of the realities of my age—domestic and international problems, public injustices, inward strains that give birth to acts of human meanness. But although I know the problems and even perhaps the "correct" solutions, I also know that this knowledge of mine lacks potency. My stored head, this kingdom—my pride, my liberalism, my feeling for human complexity—none of this alters the world; it only exhausts me with constant naggings about powerlessness. What can I do?

Pop tunes that begin "I'll Build a Stairway to the Stars" don't help much with that problem—which is to say, thirties' pop lyrics didn't link up very directly with "reality." Rock lyrics of the sixties, on the other hand, do link up—many of them. The world of the rock lyric encompasses war protest (The Fugs: "Kill for Peace"), overdue social justice (Bob Dylan: "Blowin' in the Wind"), black hippies' fury (Jimi Hendrix: "If 6 Was 9"). That world includes, in addition, intricate human relationships in which people press themselves to define their feelings precisely (The Beatles: "She Said She Said"). And it blinks neither at sexual hypocrisies (The Rolling Stones: "Back Street Girl") nor at depressing or disgusting visual details or urban scenes (John Hartford: "Shiny Rails of Steel"). Boosters of one or another rock lyric, true enough, often lose their cool. " 'Learn to forget,' " a writer says in *Crawdaddy,* quoting a snippet of a rock tune. "—what power that phrase has! It's possible to get stoned for days by listening to this song. For a while it will seem the one truth available to us . . . a catalyst with more potential for generating truth . . . than anything since middle Faulkner.")

But learn to forget boosters: rock lyrics *are* in closer touch with contemporary life than pop used to be. And it's plain that contemporary minds and rock "groove" together partly because many rock songs take cognizance of the ills that exacerbate such minds. Partly—but not wholly. The complex case is that, if one phase of the rock experience is confirmation of what a man knows, the other phase, equally telling, is escape from the knowledge. —Bring along all your views, says the rock invitation. Your liberal opinions. Your knowledge of the atrocities committed by numberless power structures of the past. Your analyst's ideas about today's oedipal hangup. Your own manipulative, categorizing, classifying, SAT braininess. You can not only cross the rock threshold bearing this paraphernalia; you can retreat to it, consult it, any time you want—by tuning back in to the lyrics. No obligation, in this pop world, to mindlessness . . . —But now if you'd *like* something else . . . If you want your freedom, if you'd care to blow your mind, shed those opinions, plunge into selflessness, into a liberating perception of the uselessness, the unavailingness, the futility of the very notion of opinionated personhood, well, it so happens to happen there's something, dig, real helpful here. . . . What is being said is that the rock invitation offers the audience a momentary chance to have it both ways: if I accept the invitation, I can simultaneously be political and beyond politics, intellectual and beyond intellectuality, independent and beyond personal independence.

I can be these contrary things because the rock experience at its most intense is an intimation of engulfment and merger, a route to a flowing, ego-transcending oneness. As fans and enemies alike know, rock sound overwhelms separatoness, the mental operations that discern and define here and there, me and not-me. (Many of the lyrics work symbolically or subliminally toward the same end.) Pounded by volume, riddled by light, the listener slides free from the restraining self and from the pretenses of a private, "unique" rationality. Preparation for the descent is of various sorts. One man may have given houseroom in his head to a desire for connection with the unconscious roots of life—D. H. Lawrence's blood being. Another, unbookish, has experienced frustration in the public world of objective laws, ethnic or money interests—learned his impatience with the procedural and the discrete outdoors, as it were. Another despises the tyranny of his "family self" or his student role. All are alike, though, in their relish for a thunderous, enveloping, self-shattering moment wherein the capacity for evaluating an otherness is itself rocked and shaken, and the mob of the senses cries out: What we feel, we are!

That this half-real, half-metaphorical self-shattering lies at the tumultuous center of the rock experience is an observation made verbally (the music itself makes it to anyone who listens) over and over, by low-cult and high-cult critics alike. Mr. Paul Williams in *Crawdaddy* remarks that "the direct appeal to the mind made by 'folk' (straightforward words, guitar, voice) cannot compare . . . to the abilities of rock to move people's goddam muscles, bodies, caught up and swaying and moving so that a phrase . . . can actually become your whole body, can sink into your soul on a more-than-cognitive level. Rock, because of the number of senses it can get to (on a dance floor, eyes, ears, nose, mouth and tactile) and the extent to which it can pervade those senses, is really the most advanced art form we have." Professor Goldman comments that, "like the effect of LSD, that of rock . . . is to spotlight [things] in a field of high concentration and merge them with the spectator in a union that is almost mystical."

And, as indicated, the rock lyricist is himself hip to the phenomenon of the "mystical union." The truth "allowable only to the very great" which Professor Poirier heard in a Beatles' song is an explicit assertion of the arbitrariness of ego separations, and of the desirability of soaring free from the mind-ridden world of subjects and objects. "I am within you and without you," these sirens call. "I am he as you are he as you are me and we are all together. . . ." The kitsch version of this "truth"—it emerges as

an endorsement of a kind of universal group-gropeism—appears
in a hundred lesser songs:

> I think it's so groovy now
> That people are finally getting together
> I think it's so wonderful—and how!—that people are finally
>   getting together
> Reach out in the darkness
> Reach out in the darkness, etc.

> [Friend and Lover: "Reach Out in the Darkness"]

And its mate is a crude symbolic vision of the nonhuman world—
the hard-edged manifold of objects, landscapes, nameable loca-
tions—as capable of losing its own stiff substance and flowing
into a dislocating unassemblable gooeyness:

> MacArthur Park is melting in the dark,
> All the sweet, green icing flowing down.
> Someone left the cake out in the rain,
> And I don't think that I can take it,
> 'Cause it took so long to bake it.
> And I'll never have the recipe again,
> Oh no.

> [Richard Harris:
> "MacArthur Park," composer, Jim Webb]

Admittedly, the point of substance here is itself slippery—hard to
keep in sight. Speak in expository prose about a mind-blowing
moment, and you tame the sensations—the obliterating seizures
of sound at a Hendrix concert or at the Electric Circus or any
multimedia discothèque—by turning them into "evidence." Speak
the rock writer's flaky, half-literate idiom, and you either over-
heat the Ineffable or identify the rock experience too directly
with the drug experience, obscuring the specific features of both
that rockers value most. ("'The End' [a Doors' composition] is
great to listen to when you're high . . . but 'Soul Kitchen' will
get you high, which is obviously much . . . more important":
Crawdaddy.) But if the point is tricky, it isn't trivial. That rock is

a mixed experience, appealing at once to my sense of my sophistication and my sense of the unavailingness of sophistication; that rock lifts from me the burden of knowing the good and yet believing my knowledge to be useless; that rock permits me to be part of others, not a mere resentful conscious self, not a perceiver harried on every side by multitudes of other conscious selves pressing their "distinct" values, opinions, interests, greeds forward into my space and notice: all these truths matter considerably. They establish that rock can possess quasi-religious force. It leads me past my self, beyond my separateness and difference into a world of continuous blinding sameness. For a bit, it stoneth me out of my mind.

Judging that trip, like judging any vision, isn't work for a journalist. But certain strengths and weaknesses stand forth in plain sight. Grown men of mind can benefit from access to an experience that shakes the grip of mentalism, allows the being to sense the world again, restores a feeling of continuity with "out there"; through it they can preserve an idea of human solidarity, as well as some consciousness of intellectual limits and a seemly general humility. For youngsters, too, as may be added, there is value in an escape from the narrow worlds of schoolhouse or family dining room into a sense of power, physicality, roughness, openness. (The prepubescent middle-class kid who sings mimetically along with Hendrix or Percy Sledge as he listens to a record is behaving much like Penrod imitating Rube in Tarkington's wonderful story. Such behavior recovers potentialities of being that are too rigidly excluded by "nice" families in the name of an arid politesse.)

At pubescent and postpubescent levels, though, overindulgence in mystical I-am-you-you-are-the-tree-the-tree-is-me self-transcendence isn't all plus signs and roses. The schooling of a maturing mind—*pace* now to self-hating academic revolutionaries—is often at its most intense, most interesting and most life-enhancing when its business is to toughen the concept of Difference, or when it is occupied with hierarchies of aesthetic, political, moral experience, or when the classroom or library effort is that of refining the imaginative power to comprehend a difficult otherness. And aptness for such studies can be weakened. Once upon a time it was weakened by what was called class prejudice —or by inherited or inculcated religious or political self-righteousness. The Mormon or the Catholic or the Grottlesex boy couldn't break out of himself, couldn't enter the "other point of view." So it was that teachers then complained about their pupils' inflexibility, incapacity to stand one place while imaginatively penetrating another. So it was that twenty years ago the great historian of science and teacher Herbert Butterfield was writing about troubles dealing with people who were so convinced that one or another historical position or figure—Oliver Cromwell, say—was "right," that they couldn't stir themselves to fathom the innerness of King Charles' head:

> [Someone] who is so much the prisoner of his ideas that he [is] forever unable to summon the imaginative sympathy to enter into the mentality of men who are not like-minded with himself—is the very antithesis of what is required in history. He is no more an historian than that man is an actor who cannot play Othello as well as King Lear—in fact, he is only like that bogus kind of actor who . . . is always the same, always only himself.

The problem for the future, perhaps, will be the appearance of a generation so rich in experience of merger and self-transcendence that to its mind Cromwell and Charles and early twenty-first century Harvard sophomores will seem all one, why so much fuss, man? A generation of characters whose problem won't be that they're always the same but that they're never the same . . . Because the self, like, man, the self is, like, an individuality, dependent on consciousness, and, like consciousness,—man, that's the trap we jumped. That was a nightmare . . . Consciousness. Like, *ugh.*

Future-mongering and solemnity are handmaids: proper to shoo them off and turn on the phonograph again—Paul singing "Here There and Everywhere"—to temper the profundum, and charm the mind back to pleasure and ease. You think as you listen: Perhaps in a way rock's too good a stuff to be wasted on youth. Or: Ridiculous, the idea that speaking a warm word for such attractive lyric inventiveness could ever corrupt a youth . . . Then you think: have to turn the volume controls all the way up for an hour before a person could even begin to approximate the whirly amiable slow-up available from two or three back-to-back joints of pot.

And then you think: sound judgment is quite impossible anyway, for it must wait until we know what's to come of us, what the next human beings will be like, what qualities will be saved and lost, what "our" future is to be. A long wait.

—But this flurry of *gentilesse* and tolerance is, as a final word, too soft. People who like the tunes but reject the salvation— moldy figs who play the music at the old sound levels and hunt for the old musical pleasures and go on making the traditional musical discriminations and persist in thinking that chaps are dotty who claim they am I and I am they—these senior types, never blowing their minds, aren't fools and may still preserve a civilized value now beleaguered on many fronts.

What value, exactly?

Just conceivably, nothing less than that of the self itself.

Mississippi Learning

In its first summer the Tougaloo Enrichment Program at Mary Holmes Junior College in West Point, Mississippi, enrolled two hundred black students from the delta counties of the state. The students were either already enrolled or about to enroll in integrated high schools. The faculty was drawn chiefly from high schools and colleges in the South; the tutorial staff, responsible for most of the teaching, consisted of undergraduates from two Massachusetts colleges (Smith and Amherst), plus several students from Negro colleges in the South. The following is from a journal kept during a short visit.

Is it any good? Are we doing anything that matters? There are troubles, speaking mildly. We have a thousand ways of naming them, but everything comes down to this: The air in the classroom is too dense—more obstacles, more currents of feeling, more contrarieties of response, more "irrelevant" emotion between student and teacher and the public than I've known before. These are not simply schoolchildren. They are always more and less than "students." Their innerness is different.

These children at most moments are exercising an extraordinary amount of self-control and are by no means unconscious of that fact themselves. Many of them are Purple Hearts now—bomb fragments from McComb, concussed heads from the baseball bats that beat people up on the first day of integrated school in Grenada. Girls and boys alike have been set on, and they expect to be set on again. They may run and get away alive, or they may not. Yet they are functioning. They're put down here amid a new community—strangers, "white oppressors"—and they go on functioning. And they know that to function in these circumstances is an accomplishment. They know that there is ground for pride in what they are, and there is some pride and even arrogance in them. The Grenada crowd, for instance—they had told their tutors they would just as soon be home this summer, because home is where the action is, more exciting and dangerous than sleepy old West Point.

A longing to provoke violence and a terror of violence and a pride in having endured it and a sullenness at seeming dependent on people who haven't endured it—all these feelings coexist in many of these heads. And the feelings don't stay out of the classroom. They come and go and thicken the air, and while you are working you suddenly feel the tightness of God knows how many membranes holding the order and calm together. The tightness—and the *thinness*.

There is a mixture of pugnacity and fear—but there's more to it than that. The tutors complain that while there are reservoirs of disaffection in their students, they—the tutors—can't tap them in class. "How is your life?" the tutor asks. "Nice," the students answer, for at school life *is* nice. It has to be. Something somewhere has to be nice. What do you think of this enrichment program? Nice, the students answer. What does it mean to be an American? Your rights are protected and you can buy more nice things, they reply. Reality is excluded by convention from the classroom; the negative spirit is kept out of this desperately needed nice place. The notion that Teacher wants to permit that negating, cynical, mocking, back-alley nature to assert itself during class, wants to bring reality—things as they are—into the school, is in some way crazy; bad manners; dumb. It's like interrupting a beautiful hymn on Sunday morning with a discussion of your old man's Saturday-night drunk. Let's keep the few clean worlds we know inviolate.

And there's no stopping even here. There is a more painful truth: Frustration among teachers and students is being fostered, purposefully exacerbated. The center of the student-teacher community at West Point isn't the administration or the white majority among the tutors; it is a nascent black-power subculture solidifying among the Negro tutors and several of the older, sharper Negro students. There is an effort to use the white tutors; to make them look foolish; to harass them for money, special privileges, and the like; to heighten suspicion of them among the students; to turn their whiteness into the Enemy. A great deal of the time, the effort amounts only to competitive ploys, acts of pettishness not thought out in advance. But at other moments private wars—open contests between whites and blacks—actually break out. And these wars are obstacles or barriers that, once again, can't be thought of as having a place in the normal transactions called "teaching" and "learning."

How can I make the point less abstract? There is no choice except to talk about my own brief, private war—and about the feelings I thought were engaged in it. (I believe that war had a lot in common with others being waged at West Point.)

Who was my opponent? Calver Jackson, I'll call him—Negro tutor, intelligent, twenty-two, chief SNCC organizer in —— County, Alabama. How far can I go in offering the character of C.J.? How much do I know? I've spent time brooding about him, I'll say that—my black challenge. The day I arrived voice after voice seemed to be talking about C.J.: "That's C.J."; "C.J.'s just plain marvelous." Another voice I remember said: "C.J. just hates us. You never know where you are with him. Sometimes he's awfully nice. But that's rare, really. He hates us, really. It's terrible. He makes them all hate us."

C.J. is about five foot eleven, rather chubby, light on his feet, very black, with very quick eyes—more menace than humor in them—handsome features tending toward sulkiness, movements suggesting reluctance to waste any physical energy, and a faint swagger in his walk. According to C.J. you lose your figure when you go to work for SNCC—too sedentary. The kids say C.J. was quarterback of his high school football team for three years, star basketball player in college, etc. I watched him play basketball. He gave away five years and more to the other players, and the game is played hard. C.J. is a playmaker, court general, brilliant passer, sizer-up of situations, etc. His shooting eye has gone, but I record, for the truth of it, that he sank—surprising everyone—a fine outside jumper that iced the game for his team. It was Skins vs. Shirts, and C.J. played in a weird, slickerish jacket that he wore to sweat off blubber. There was constant communication with him from the sidelines; the kids ceaselessly called out to him: "Hey, C.J. C.J., how about this, how about that . . . ?"

He looks past you when you are introduced. He nods at you when he comes into your party. He doesn't stay long. He talks a good deal, outdoors, to the other Negro tutors and to the tutorial groups. He is said to be irresponsible, and there's something to this. He drives wildly with a dozen kids in the back of the project's rented station wagons, taking them to the swimming pool in Starkville. (West Point had a pool, but when an integration move was made, the town simply filled it with sand. So you drive fifteen miles over back roads to Starkville where there's money, hence an integrated pool—meaning open to Negroes and whites, but whites don't come, having access to private pools.) C.J. drives wildly and is admired as a hero by the younger lads, as he is admired as a daring lover by the girls.

What placed C.J. in a private contest with me? The professors who preceded me at West Point, the white ones, apparently were badly briefed and ill-informed about the audience. They gave abstract talks about economic determinism. They explained NATO and the Common Market, etc., at a level that implied that all two hundred children were subscribers to *The New York Times*. Maybe they were worried about seeming to condescend. In any case, their deficiencies provoked the Negro tutors into taunting the white tutors about the irrelevance and fatuity of their instructors. The white tutors who knew me retaliated by puffing me as a white hope. Maybe the other professors were abstract or irrelevant, but I wouldn't be. I was this; I was that.

They could speak with great confidence because they planned to get to me the minute I arrived, fill me in, tell me what to do and say. They did just that the night I came in.

How did it work out? If it was a contest, who won? As always in life, nobody won: Death and pain and accident interfered—turned the whole idea of a contest into an ugly joke. I record in passing—a stroke of vanity that I gave the best performance of my life in a public lecture, doing the history of a blues note, moving from weary blues and boogie-woogie through to Langston Hughes and on to Ralph Ellison, telling what the blues expressed and why the thing expressed is a mass feeling, talking about the Negro writer's struggle to create a language capable of expressing more than a mass feeling, more than the blues sense that nobody can win, capable of articulating an individual response. It was an antiblues talk; it invoked Ellison's hero, Louis Armstrong, as expander and transcender of the blues; it was rabble-rousing and self-dramatizing and funny.

I shouted some blues and played some on the auditorium piano, and they shouted with me. They wanted more, and I taunted them by saying that it's all too imitable; the world is full of blues-doers, people white and black and Japanese. We want a man to inhabit his own skin, name his own feelings, have his own response to the world. Having your own responses is being free. Pure blues is a jail to be broken, etc.

It was damned good. And at the very moment I was thinking how damned good, one of our station wagons was piling up on a back road: one student was killed and several were badly injured. Possibly the wagon had been tailgated; that had happened often—revenge by rednecks against Negroes driving shiny cars with a white girl aboard. It was an ambiguous accident and a bad moment for the program. I am not speaking about the poor torn-up kids—who in my position can say anything here? The director came out of the hospital with personal belongings to be returned to the dead lad's parents—in exchange for fostering his ambition, they got a pencil box (the thing was so dear to the boy that he took it everywhere with him, even to the swimming pool), unbroken glasses, and a swim suit. The project hung on the edge of hysteria that night.

I taught the next morning, and I didn't think much about the dead lad (I didn't know him, if that's an excuse) once the memorial service was over. Why was this so? Partly because C.J. was in my class. I had by now taught the whole cycle—eight English classes—gradually improving as I went because I had learned how to start closer to where they seemed to be. During this class, C.J. and I were in a running wordless dialogue. C.J. sat in the back row—not with the three other tutors but by himself. Everyone was suppressed and edgy in the aftermath of the accident. C.J. sat in back and spoke not a word. He opened a comic book and stared down at it—an expression of contempt. Whenever I looked his way quickly during that class, I caught his eye. Instantly, he looked down angrily, pretending he had not been listening and would not dream of listening, that he was bored.

At the end of the hour, when I had the ritual conversation with the tutors, asking them what they would be doing in English hour that afternoon and giving them suggestions, C.J. said abruptly, "We ain't meetin', my group." I felt the resistance, the wall, the antipathy, and I was with the sweet-faced Smith girl who said they hate us. But, of course, my mind wouldn't cut out altogether. It thought by habit, as the younger people's minds probably didn't. It told me first, repetitiously and piously, that exactly this militancy and intransigence were what was desperately needed.

Then habit went further. It said there was personal jealousy in the equation. C.J. was charismatic in his community, and my students presented me as charismatic in mine. My blues lecture the day before did impinge, did move onto his turf. Two little girls from the newspaper had interviewed me. They asked if I would play afterward (nobody yet knew of the accident). There was cheering, applause, etc. So here was a stranger on C.J.'s turf who wasn't quite as easily put down, because fortunately he had been warned about being abstract before he opened his mouth.

And then my mind said to consider the class, too. Consider the feelings that must have been there in the room as I worked—not just the standard continuum of pride, fear, shame, etc., or guilt and anger about the little boy killed. But look at what this time must have been like for C.J.—and for several others in the class. I had been talking about a poem called "Florida Road Workers" by Langston Hughes. My opening ploy had been to change the meaning of a word by changing the way it was said—the little idea being to help them see the need to act out poems, act through the words. A word changes meaning according to the music you play it in with your voice. We began by going up and down a row of kids asking for five different hellos, and I got some funny ones—a wary telephone hello, a chaser's hello, salesman's greeting, etc. The little idea was that to say the right hello, you have to know the situation: who's speaking, when, why, and so on. Similarly, reading a poem means knowing not just words but events and people and how human beings feel—in particular, the human being saying the poem—in various circumstances.

I said there were some words the Florida road worker says that are like hello in the sense that you have to hear the music that goes with the word. But I suggested that we read and enjoy it, and then we could worry about that:

Florida Road Workers

I'm makin' a road
For the cars to fly by on,
Makin' a road
Through the palmetto thicket
For light and civilization
To travel on.

I'm makin' a road
For the rich to sweep over
In their big cars
And leave me standin' here.

Sure,
A road helps everybody!
Rich folks ride—
And I get to see 'em ride.

I ain't never seen nobody
Ride so fine before.
Hey, Buddy! Look!
I'm makin' a road!

I asked for some readers, and all the readings were straight. The taunting, ironic thing in the worker's voice—"Hey, Buddy!" or "Sure"—wasn't in the room. So I started on a lad in the front and asked if he means what he's saying, this worker, when he says a road helps everybody. Usual moment: Will the school-church never-never-land be opened to reality or won't it? C.J.'s head was up, listening. I didn't show that I knew this. Yes, the youngster said, he means it. He does? I said incredulously. How so? Why? What do you mean? Well, the boy said, it's just true, that's all. The road is good for the white man to ride on, and it's good for the Negro to look at him. I was stopped momentarily. Was the boy putting me on? No, clearly not. I looked up; C.J.'s eyes were down again, but I thought I touched some fury in him.

Now the class started. I tried to get somebody to feel that the man is not in love with his job or with the world. It took time and teacherly moves and hints and leads and lots of lousy stuff and some breaks, and I felt everybody holding his temper and patience, including me. We were all relieved as hell when at last a student said that the worker is mad: It's not the same to ride as to watch; he's making a mad joke; you could make "Sure" pretty fierce and sneering—"really hot"—and be right. And when all this came, it came with a lovely breaking surge. When they saw, they *saw!* They turned around and looked at each other, absolutely delighted; they were in the game, impressed—very up. I felt exhilarated in their exhilaration. It mattered.

But, I told myself, think what obstacles to the teaching job could have been in that room. Cross over into C.J.'s head. What an exacerbation, what a humiliation, what an infuriation those moments must have been. Here's the white man; see him trying to "explain"—to the Negro—a Negro's helpless self-mocking rage at the exploitation of the Negro. See the friendly white man taking up the black man's cause and trying to be patient about getting the nature of this complaint across. And no doubt thinking, somewhere in him, My God, they really are dumb, aren't they, the niggers? They don't get anything.

So C.J. had to watch this—a white man scratching at this job, and all the while sapping the potential and necessary energies of hatred in the blacks before him. Maybe—if he were just a shade less self-absorbed than I thought he was—maybe C.J. suffered, watching the soul brothers stumble around, missing the point, having to be shown it.

Then I had another feeling. Why should a white man be there at all at this spectacle, claiming to understand a pain he never shared? Why should he understand, interpret, carry over—every part of it involving placing himself in a superior position, standing forth as their superior, the man with magic.

You have no right to see yourself standing there in the role of the teacher, they say to themselves. You have nothing to teach us. What does it matter what some trick of irony comes to in a poem? We know the beating beyond the words. We watched the cars. We were there. Our fathers were beaten and exploited. We were beaten. Things, not words. And if we can't master the symbols, the black marks, we have felt the clubs and the knives and the pickax and the heat.

So, man, get out of my way, we ain't going to meet.

And here I am, aware of this sullen fury bent on me, and not just aware of it but educated by it. By everything that's right, by everything these kids have endured as children, by all they stand to endure next week, month, their whole lives, they possess an inherent claim to dignity and value that surpasses Teacher's, no matter how smart or good he says he is. In absolute moral terms, in terms of balance and courage and patience and humor—God knows they are better creatures than I am, with more substance, more truth in them.

And the point is that these strains—these seeings and counterseeings and tensions of self-assessment—are going on *in a classroom*. I am not only teaching—I see over to the far side of the moon and grasp for a moment the absurdity of this kind of "leading out"—leading out into the white world of invented agonies, invented tranquilizers, invented puzzles. I saw my puerility, my helplessness. I saw that the culture I lead them toward knows less than it claims to. Our "grading them up" is a kind of minor epicicular correction, not a fundamental offering of light. The world stopped for that second, I was on edge. I even knew at that instant that part of C.J.'s feeling was a kind of shame at himself, for being mean to us when we can't know any better, when we are at least trying to understand, trying to care as many do not. Listen to me, listen, I forgive you, you white bastard, but just get out, will you?

And, finally, what did I want to do when I saw all this? I wanted to *say* I saw it; I wanted to turn it into talk, into a discovery, into something to note down in a journal. Marvelous! Hey, buddy, I get it! Jesus Christ, look at me, I'm building a piece of prose! I get it! *Can* I possibly get anything? I'm leaving. I'm white and I'm always going to be leaving. I'm always going to be thinking it into a set of complexities, naming them off, feeling better for the names, and then clearing out and forgetting the experience. Hey, buddy! White man! Leave us alone; *we ain't going to meet.*

All right, a bit overheated. C.J. and I never traded blows, after all. The day I left he said a sulky good-bye (he spoke first, I noted childishly in my pride) from behind half a pickup truck. The main point—I repeat it—is that these classrooms and these situations were crowded. Every kind of human tide crossing and meeting, buzzing, a thousand kinds of feeling. I would say the teaching, as teaching, went much slower than usual. I would also say that there is more in it for the teacher. He feels himself being read as he reads. The light comes and goes in his students. Apathy and stoniness put it out. There are fantasies and longing. Then it comes to life again. People are sometimes unbelievably quick. There was a lot in this for us, and our kids knew it. They tended to want to hang around there. A white Alabaman on the faculty said to me, "Listen, if I didn't have kids like these on the weekend to work with during the year, I don't know where I'd get my strength."

And that's what I got, too: strength. It wasn't from some cliché about Negro vitality. And it wasn't from some self-inflating sense of *noblesse oblige;* if I have quadratics and alphabet skills, I share them because I am "nice." No, the strength comes from the infusion of certainty. And that's my last "observation." It is about the gift of certainty—knowing where you are, knowing what's right and wrong—that is an amazing experience.

You go there and you understand for the first time—clearly, if you're like me—that there are some things on earth that must be changed. They simply must and simply will. You are rich in the understanding of necessity and potency and rightness. (Beatings are wrong. Ignorance of exploitation is wrong.) You know for the first time that certain events must occur and that you and others are going to make them occur, or at least are going to work to make them occur. You see that revolution is not a word but a pointing toward what obviously, absolutely must happen, and you are lifted up by this sight, by the freshening awareness of how criminally wrong a wrong can be *known* to be by a mere human being—namely, yourself. And knowing all this, knowing that the real "success" for the white teacher is to end up for a while on the receiving end of hate, you plan to work out a way to come back.

The Age of Overkill

The Spirit of Overkill was everywhere in this period. Drifting sluggishly over the land from the international power struggle, a dense, polluting wave, it penetrated the very marrow of the culture. Journalism, conversation, manners, the arts—the innermost thoughts and feelings of men—all were touched or tainted.

At first the influence appeared only in certain small changes of accent and idiom, hints of the habitual irascibility to come. The emergence of anger as the normal Anglo-American tone of voice was scarcely noticed. But in the sequel the whole age was caught up in verbal ferocity, and at the climax, in the late sixties, the fury turned compulsive. In speech and song, poem and proclamation, fiercely, ceaselessly, a weird, inexplicable "assault" was pressed—not at new "enemies" but at old ones already in tatters. There was no breaking out of the mindless cycle of supertaunts; long after the target institutions lay in lifeless ruin at their feet, men continued to rain down abuse upon them, locked in the rage to rage. And at the end, crazed by hatred that could find no standing object to destroy, they beat and tore at themselves.

As might be guessed, the movement at its height was marked by episodes of uncommon vulgarity and tastelessness. One periodical of the day—its motto was "Irreverence is our only sacred cow"—published a "report" on President Lyndon Johnson's behavior on the Air Force plane that bore him back to Washington from Dallas after the assassination of President Kennedy; it asserted that the President, before taking the oath, had mounted the casket and reached sexual climax in the throat wound of his dead predecessor (*The Realist*, 1967). Another—a Methodist church magazine, which lusted, like the secular organs of the time, after new modes of mockery—another invented a news-story framework for the nineteenth-century Nietzschean cry that "God is dead," and "quoted" the reactions of the crude and witless groat to the "item." The Pope: ". . . it is difficult to imagine how we shall proceed without Him." De Gaulle: "God is dead! Long live France!" President Truman: "I'm always sorry to hear somebody is dead. It's a damn shame." President Eisenhower: "He will be missed" (*Motive*, 1966).

More interesting than the vulgarity at full tide, however, was the power of Overkill throughout its span to draw together ill-sorted minds. The decade's steady hounding of people "over thirty" was led, for the most part, by public entertainers, "rock groups," and the like. Beatle Harrison spoke against "all these old fools who are governing us and . . . bombing us and doin' all that. . . ." Stone Jagger laid it down: "Politics, like the legal system, is dominated by old men. Old men who are also bugged by religion." Leary of Milbrook, a guru, told undergraduates at Yale: "Your legislators, your President, and your Defense Department are for the most part impotent old men who are riding on youth. They don't want you to be free. Laws are made by old people who don't want young people to do exactly those things young people were meant to do—to make love, turn on, and have a good time" (*Friday*, 1968).

But in the very season that Stones and Beatles and gurus were thus baying the aged, a respected Nobel Prize winner himself elected to run with the pack. At the time I did my best work, said Dr. James Watson to an undergraduate audience of hundreds at Harvard (the time was the spring of 1968), "I thought of people over forty as at the end of their lives . . . and that was the right attitude to take—not too much reverence for the big boys. If they knew what to do, they'd be doing it."

And Professor Watson was but one of hundreds of distinguished figures from the world of mind who lent weight to the

Overkill cause. From the first, indeed, that cause was a favorite with artists as well as intellectuals. James Baldwin, the novelist and essayist, spoke authentic Overkill whenever he appeared in public. (The author of *Another Country* was given to describing his country as "the Fourth Reich": *New York Times*, 1968.) Susan Sontag, a writer well known in that day, was no less fiercely ignorant in her essays on history and race: "The white race is the cancer of history," she said flatly. "It is the white race and it alone—its ideologies and inventions—which eradicates autonomous civilization wherever it spreads, which has upset the ecological balance of the planet, which now threatens the very existence of life itself" (*Partisan Review*, 1967).

Given leadership of this order, youth inevitably responded with explosions of its own—student editorials calling for guerrilla bands to roar through "college campuses burning books, burning degrees and exams, burning school records, busting up class-rooms, and freeing our brothers from the prison of the univer-sity . . ." The Berkeley *Barb* continued: "The universities cannot be reformed. They must be abandoned or closed down. They should be used as bases for actions against society, but never taken seriously. The professors have nothing to teach. . . . We can learn more from any jail than we can from any university." And the result was, to repeat, that by the end of the sixties the entire articulate Anglo-American community—young, middle-aged, and aged people alike—was transformed into a monster-chorus of damnation-dealers, its single voice pitched ever at hysterical level, its prime aim to transform every form of dis-course into a blast.

There were Overkill aphorisms in that period ("The world belongs to politics, which is to say the world belongs to death": Theodore Roszak), and Overkill definitions ("The family is the American fascism": Paul Goodman). There were Overkill toppers, comebacks, and sneers. (When a television interviewer in England told the novelist Mary McCarthy that she appeared to be "accusing [the American] people of stupidity, not wicked-ness," the author stoutly replied, "I think they are wicked, too.")

There were Overkill critical assessments (Thomas Wolfe was a "professional hillbilly": Alfred Kazin), and Overkill letters to the editor, especially in the Manhattan weeklies of the day. "We are rats in a laboratory maze," the letter writers regularly wrote in. "The Government is feeding us frustration, bringing us to the verge of madness." (Replies to these letters were themselves similarly tinged. One columnist for a suburban paper called *Newsday* answered his mail by stamping the letters with an obscenity—special oversized rubber stamp—and returning them straight to their senders.) There was Overkill in public speaking, sometimes in rhetorical questions ("You call yourselves revolutionaries?" shouted Rap Brown. "How many white folks you killed today?"), sometimes in hymns of praise ("All the people at the Pentagon!" shouted the poet Allen Ginsberg, honoring the turned-on tastes of a group of peace marchers. "They were all heads!"), sometimes in historical analogies ("Reading a speech of Andrew Jackson's . . . the other day," said Robert Bly, declining a prize at the 1968 National Book Awards, "I realized he was the Westmoreland of 1830").

And there were reams—floods—oceans of Overkill poetry. New chants were reported in newspapers. ("Dean Rusk is a murderer!" shouted four hundred in unison outside a West Coast hotel.) Simple Overkill refrains were "socko" Off Broadway. ("The middle class/ Are just like pigs . . . The middle class/ Are just like pigs": Jacques Brel.) Old-style blues underwent sea changes: "My Baby Done Left Me and I Feel Like Home-made Shit": The Fugs.

And prose poems of immeasurable putridity took art straight to its borders—witness the garbage epic by a Mrs. Hentoff, columnist for a paper called *The Village Voice*. The theme of the work—New York *as* garbage—was a response to a lengthy strike by city garbage collectors early in 1968. The opening strains sang softly and with satisfaction of Manhattan sans sanitation. (". . . almost as if [the city] had become what we knew it was all along. There was garbage on the sidewalks, garbage in the gutters, garbage lining the walls of buildings, garbage blowing in the wind . . .") Then, to a moving ripe air, the voice rose in a plea that the strike never be ended, that it go "on and on until the garbage fill[s] the canyons and the rats leap from mound to mound." And finally, at the close, a gentle self-loving cadence celebrated the poet's "truthful image" of the town.*

Contemporary observers who maintained critical detachment from the new fashion, and sought to define its relations with the past, turned up several notions that still possess interest. One writer theorized that Overkill was an extension of the American tall-tale tradition. Another traced its genesis to the post-nineteenth-century expansion of literacy and general education, developments that intensified a threat to the elite. (According to this view, men who considered themselves to belong to the elite were obliged to speak and write in extravagant terms in order to establish their position. In ages of limited literacy, this was unnecessary; a man possessing the ability to order his thoughts cogently on paper was an aristocrat by virtue of that ability. But once cogency was brought within Everyman's reach, it ceased to be a distinction: wildness had to come in.)

Still other theorists sought to connect the advent of Overkill with the new educational theories of the time. "Think," wrote one observer, "think of the uphill fifty-year struggle waged by educators on behalf of 'immediacy' and 'relevance' as against knowledge and the sense of the past. Is no measure of credit owing here? Suppose for a moment that, in place of new-style utter nowsense, children were still immersed in the dreary stuff of history:

---

* Another Overkill salute, by an American poet, to New York filth can be found in the Russian poet Yevgeny Yevtushenko's poem "Smog," which detailed a trip to America in the 1960s. Yevtushenko quoted Robert Lowell as having explained city soot as "a vengeance from heaven for depravity and moral collapse." It is worth noting, perhaps, as a curiosity, that the Russian poet appears to have picked up a taste for Overkill idiom during the trip in question. In the same poem he saw a likeness between his accommodations at the Chelsea Hotel on Eighth Avenue and Twenty-third Street and a concentration camp. ("In the cell-like room," he wrote, "there is a smell of Dachau.")

could the thrust of a story of Western Civilization like Miss Sontag's [see above] ever then have been felt?"

But though a few contemporary theses or "explanations" retain an edge of usefulness, most were error-strewn. It was usual, for instance, to date abuse-escalation in the late sixties, coincident with the Southeast Asian wars, and to ignore the embryonic states, as well as sudden prophetic outbursts like Lord Russell's against Macmillan and Kennedy:

> We used to call Hitler wicked for killing off the Jews, but Kennedy and Macmillan are much more wicked than Hitler. . . . We cannot obey these murderers. They are wicked. They are abominable. They are the wickedest people who ever lived in the history of man and it is our duty to do what we can against them. *

Again: a standard practice was to associate verbal extravagance and apocalyptic expression primarily with the political left—new militants, student activists, Filthy Speech chiefs, and the rest. It was an understandable mistake: many public events that attracted notice were reported in ways that nourished acceptance of the equation. A writer for *The New Yorker* magazine attending a young people's political convention in Chicago in 1967 observed that, for a whole week, the word *revolution* was used "for every nuance of dissent."

Yet even so it must remain mystifying that, on the basis of slim evidence like this, men could conclude that Overkill was an identifying mark of the left. Before Berkeley there were the so-called Birchers, radical rightists apt at every form of verbal excess. ("The whole country is one vast insane asylum and they're letting the worst patients run the place": Robert Welch, founder of the Birch Society.) And could it really have been believed that, say, Norman Mailer (another writer well regarded

---

* In 1961. Lord Russell's name is another reminder of a point worth stressing: many foreigners learned to speak Overkill with ease. Not least notable of them was Fidel Castro, who produced much classic work—including a jibe (at the 1968 International Cultural Congress at Havana) at population-control programs. Such programs, the Cuban premier asserted, were proof of "imperialism's lack of faith in the future."

in this period) on the American narcosis was in any significant sense different from the 1967 Christian Crusade's Dean Noebel, who held forth as follows on the "Commie-Beatle Pact"? ". . . the Communists have contrived an elaborate, calculating and scientific technique directed at rendering a generation of American youth useless through nerve-jamming, mental deterioration and retardation. . . . The destructive music of the Beatles . . . reinforces . . . mental breakdown. . . ."

The truth that should have been plain even then was that Overkill was larger than politics: Overkill masters cared far more for style than for views. The issue of *The Realist* that carried the report on the behavior of President Johnson also contained an account—equally slanderous—of President Kennedy as a client of Dallas call girls. And there was the celebrated Kopkind case, involving a correspondent in Washington for an English leftist weekly. Though yielding to no man in his detestation of President Johnson, the correspondent Kopkind was haunted (apparently) by an even deeper passion—that for Overkill—and he spoke the tongue continually, even when no one hateful was by. ("Senator [Eugene] McCarthy is one of the Senate's few intellectuals," wrote this pundit, "and . . . one of its most obvious hypocrites: the two go hand in hand.")

And if the movement was larger than politics, it was also—dare we say?—more complex than the conventional wisdom of our own day even yet allows. "Despondent over their inability to alter the course of national affairs, men turned in helpless fury to a vocabulary of imprecation which they themselves knew to be useless, but that at least permitted an expression of agony, of fierce frustration, of certainty that apocalypse was near." Here is the genetic thesis in favor just now; it is attractive, and when pressed in connection with certain literary heroes of that time—rare men whose integrity matched their intensity—it may be held to contain a piece of the truth.

But surely we oversimplify if we consider impotence to be the single key. The route to satisfactory accounts of broad cultural movements passes invariably through thickets of complication.

And in travelling that path, there is some point always in attending to primary meanings. In the time of which we speak, the term *Overkill* referred to surplus obliterative power—mega-weapons capable of killing ten times the human population and turning the earth to ashes thrice. And implicit in the surplus, as in certain usages of the word, was the assumption that lives destroyed still await destruction and are thus in some inexpressible sense unreal. (A man's third death can be counted as well as his first.) Putting it another way: When obliterative power is adjusted to the sum of the obliterable, that adjustment constitutes an acknowledgment of the reality of existence. But when there is no such adjustment, when men ignore the sum of the obliterable, when men manufacture destruction beyond what is "needed," it is a sign of a weakened sense of the hard, substantial, objective world.

And precisely that weakness figured, as we must now recognize, in Overkill as a *cultural* phenomenon. It is in fact possible that this element alone—the loss of belief in a substantive outer reality—separated the Overkillers of the sixties from premodern titans of abuse. The heroic scorners of earlier times—Dante on to Swift—had no more energy of contempt than late twentieth-century man. But they did have a far stronger conviction that beyond them lay living targets, villains whose substance words could touch and wound. ("Vilify! Vilify!" went Beaumarchais's famous aphorism. "At least some of the dirt *will stick.*") Even the cooler arguefiers of the pre-Overkill past dwelt on the substantiality of the world inhabited by their enemies, and upon the necessity of imaginatively penetrating that world in order to hurt. William James, for one, never tired of quoting a contemporary who insisted that the first duty of men with the pacifist conscience was to "enter the point of view of the militarist and seek to move the point." Everywhere in former days the clearly held assumption was that the "opponent" did exist.

But in the sixties—to say it once again—a frail sense of outer reality had become the rule: a disbelief in counterunderstandings of events that pit themselves over against mine. The disbelief

showed itself not only in Overkill spectaculars—the notorious fits
of fury that plucked out eyes from severed heads. It appeared
also in the frequency of theatrical metaphor in Overkill masters'
chat. All England is an empty music hall, cried the playwright
John Osborne, as the curtain rose on the Overkill age. "On the
Vietnam stage," said the editor of the New Statesman at the end
of the decade, "the West enacts a travesty of itself, spoken in
Newspeak, performed by fake heroes and real buffoons. . . ."
And these writers only echoed the common American line. "The
stars of Vietnam," wrote a critic on The Village Voice, "are LBJ
and Ho, Westmoreland and Giap . . . they are all playing the
parts. . . . Senator Eugene McCarthy, waiting in the wings for a
piece of scenery to fall on the actor he is understudying . . .
Senator Robert F. Kennedy . . . in his dressing room . . . this
multi-billion dollar superproduction . . ." Ceaselessly the Voice
of Overkill chanted to itself that there was nothing substantial
Out There. The bad men were shadows, not substances; mere
actors, figures in shows, not penetrable, imaginable bodies, not
men who thought and felt their way into their mistakes. The
likelihood is, in sum, that the Overkill phenomenon is best
thought of as part of a seamless cultural whole embracing even
the astrophysics of that day—that incredible world view wherein,
as one critical contemporary (Hannah Arendt) wrote, "instead of
objective qualities . . . we find instruments, and instead of
nature or the universe . . . [the investigator] encounters only
himself."

But, as must be added, the latter is of course only "a likelihood"—not a certainty. The historian's voice speaks confidently,
bent on establishing once more that no corridor of the past is
beyond reach, no puzzle beyond solution. But questions nag.
Mysteries remain. The age we study was not, after all, composed
of innocents. Scholars then were no less aware than ourselves
that in periods of strife violence is done upon language. Then, as
now, sober heads could read Thucydides on the confusions of
meaning and the transformation of terms during social up-
heavals. (During the Corcyrean Revolution, said the great man,

"reckless audacity became courage . . . prudent hesitation, specious cowardice, ability to see all sides of a question inaptness to act on any. Frantic violence became the attribute of manliness; safe plotting, a justifiable means of self-defense.") And there were writers closer to the sixties in time—the Englishman Orwell, for one—who insisted on the obligation of men of mind to guard against pollution of meaning traceable either to political flatulence or intensity.

Yet in the sixties men of mind were heedless. Why so? Can any of our confidently advanced explanations finally tell us much? What were the sacred texts that misled thinkers in that day? Was it that they believed, perhaps, with the aesthete Cyril Connolly, that henceforth there would be no means of judging a man save by "the quality of his despair"? Did they therefore drive themselves into fury because fury—however abstract, frustrating, unfocused—seemed a possible substitute for moral clarity and worth? Or are we simply to conclude that verbal dementia was only the other side of the coin of physical violence—a mere necessitous counterpart to assassination, riot, arson?

If we cannot know the answers—history has cunning passages —we can at least pause to ponder our ignorance. And it will not be amiss if, as we do so, we turn again, with a freshly grateful eye, to those never sufficiently praised architects of the Great Disengagement at the century's end. But for their genius, their determination to negotiate a defusing of The Words as well as of The Bombs, what would our future now be? Who among us, reader or writer, can doubt—given the truth of what nearly happened in the sixties—that it is to their decision to lay down the lash of language that we today owe the breath of our life?

Tickle-Touch Theater:
A Reservation

"It was so wonderful," said our hostess happily—the bright-eyed girl, in the yellow velvet hostess skirt, near the punch bowl. She'd been to a performance by the Becks' Living Theater that afternoon. "The girls were scared but it only took a minute. He spoke to them twice and right away they were up on their feet and out in the aisles. Completely into it—free, being what they wanted to be. It's the future, really. They adored it!"

The Becks were in the provinces again, bringing the drama of participation to our neighbor college (Smith), exciting the entire valley. And though the idea of fencing with their rooters came to mind, it didn't stick. *Why so combative?* says the inner voice. *Can't relax and share somebody else's pleasures? Twenty years a prof and still lusting to set people straight? You actually think the Becks are far out?* For longer than a decade, after all, most of the shows that have pulled people from Snowville to the city—*The Connection* was first—have *used* the spectator, set him in a highly self-conscious relation to events "onstage," even threatened to bust or devour him.

What's more, the mod plays that turn up on litry reading lists—the ones about which it seems decent to say Something Important Started Here—invariably invented new tricks of anti-illusion, teased a picture-frame convention or tromped on spectator space. ("Those lady musicians sitting onstage in the Berliner Ensemble production of *The Caucasian Chalk Circle*— you do see the Milestone there, don't you, Student? —When they

82

come out, sit down and then *smile* at the audience, completely aware of us and cozily reminding us we are at a show?")

And then, beyond these items of firsthand knowledge, there are a hundred more known through rumor or gossip about games insiders play, Off-Off-Off bits, radical theater and dance-theater materials and attitudes. During a visit here last fall, the Polish Theater Lab director, Jerzy Grotowski, kept telling New York interviewers about a production of Marlowe's *Dr. Faustus* in which the spectators sat around a long table with Faustus (impromptu questions were addressed to them), and about another, odder pre-*Marat/Sade* production of *Kordian* (1960): "We transformed the [theater] space into an insane asylum. The entire room became a hospital with beds and so on. The actors were on the beds along with the spectators. The actors were either doctors or patients, the most interesting cases. The doctors treated the spectators as also sick. Those spectators who were treated as patients were furious—the others were very proud because they had been judged 'sane.' "

On a different front there are the famous Ann Halprin "myths" as performed in the San Francisco Dancers Workshop Company studios by dancers and audiences. Consider "Myth Seven: Carry":

> People—not, for this performance, defined as audience—entered the performance area and sat on high levels. Drums were playing and they sat facing each other and looked at one another for a long time.
>
> The director then asked, "Would anyone volunteer to choose a person and carry him through this passage?" After a pause, a man jumped down, selected a girl, and very simply carried her, and the drumming rhythm, the lights, and the carry action began to work together. This kind of activity continued very simply and began to include "Will two people carry one person?" "Will five people carry two people?" etc.
>
> New direction was added on the spot as a result of what was happening. "Will those of you who want to be carried stand in the passage and wait?" After much waiting: "Will those who volunteer

carry those who want to be carried?" People realized the primitive, archetypal connotations of this act (carried in the womb, bride carried across threshold, pope carried to alter [sic], corpse carried to grave, etc.) and the scene, especially when it seemed to resemble a Bacchanalia, was suffused with a ritualistic quality. The event concluded with an action that involved everyone either carrying or being carried. . . .

Or (yet more exotica), consider theater on the model of Allen Kaprow's *Self-Sacrifice*, advertised as "a piece without spectators," but in reality a list of "activities" to be performed by the likes of you and me, amidst the other business of our "normal lives." Activities proposed for Boston and roundabouts included these:

> For a few moments at night, shouts, words, calls, all through bullhorns. Voices moving on the streets, from windows, around corners, in hallways, alleys.
> Cars drive into filling station, erupt with white foam pouring from windows.
> People tie tar paper around many cars in supermarket lot.
> On another day, twenty or more flash-gun cameras shoot off at same time all over supermarket; shopping resumed.

Think of all this, repeat, and then come back to the Becks and the velvet hostess celebrating them, and ask yourself, Why so chuckly, chum? Whence that scratchiness, that impulse to frown and squirm?

The answer isn't that the impulse is rooted in the comic sense, though it must be said that hilarious passages do occur in some descriptions of these projects. (One Halprin dancer, for instance, has been quoted as saying that "at first it was beautiful when I was carried, but it went on and on, and I felt I was being used." Another said, "I find it hard to be really open with guys from the outside. They were kind of horny. They got me up tight." Miss Halprin's answer to the first dancer was, "Well, they didn't understand the body." To the second, she said, "They usually get horny when the lights go off.") Neither is the answer that the notion of an exchange of space and roles between performers and audience is inherently ridiculous, or that it's a Demeaning Thing when some god from the machine is lowered onto the stage—as in the Firehouse Theater's *Iphigenia Transformed* (1966)— bringing four cases of beer for an actor-spectator blast. The effort of the so-called environmental theater to dynamize theatrical interiors is fascinating as often as it is loony, and the whole tickle-touch body-contact school of dramatic production induces a kind of anxiety that's conceivably stimulating to certain types of self-bound heads.

No, the reservations come simply because the assumptions built into the rhetoric or ecstasy of enthusiasts of the new troupes and inventors—assumptions about spectator life in the old-style theater—often seen tendentious at best and at worst libelous, woolly, and dumb. What are these assumptions? One (see the velvet lady) is that the trad playgoer is a passive blob—a standing or sitting vessel that doesn't "do" but merely "receives," is blown upon or poured into. Another assumption (see Richard Schechner's "Six Axioms" for experimental theater in the Spring 1968 *TDR*) is that the central truth about the trad audience is a truth of inhibition: "they bring to the theater a decorum that has been learned elsewhere but which is nevertheless scrupulously applied here," with the result that the main audience occupation in a theater is the maintenance of Proper Tone.

Yet another assumption—more famous but not less simplistic— can be summoned by reference to Brecht's postscript to *The Rise and Fall of the City of Mahagonny,* wherein this genius distinguishes his theater, which presses the spectator to "make decisions," from the traditional theater, which asks the spectator to enlarge his empathic responses. (In the *Little Organon for the Theater,* Brecht asks, "How long are our souls going to have to leave our 'gross' bodies under cover of darkness to penetrate into those dream figures up on the rostrum . . . ?")

Spelling out persuasively, in a paragraph, what's wrong with such formulations is, needless to say, no job for a party fencer— no matter how combative-portentous his nature. It demands intuitive knowledge of the mystery of collaborative creation, the process by which the spectator himself becomes a maker and inventor and unfolder of character, an intelligence engaged in simultaneities of sympathy and judgment, one who penetrates (by quickness of mind and feeling) the actor's dream of a character, and constructs, out of gestures and shadings and restraints and inflections, a clear "imagination of an imagination," a firm map of another human being's inwardness. Great men have sat to the task of describing this process—Whitman and Tolstoy, for example, are superb on the *reader's* act of creation. And at least one uncommon mind—Péguy—has gone on to point to the palpable truth, namely, that exact counterparts to a reader's activity exist everywhere in the arts, whether in the rendering of a dramatic scene or painting or piece of sculpture or song. A "reading of a poem," says Péguy, is a joint act—call it the act of reading and being read—performed by the work and the reader, and a play is a joint act or common operation of dramatic work and spectator. And passivity is never in question, for the spectator or reader is ceaselessly "entering into" the source of the work, bending himself with sympathy and complaisance and love toward its innerness, yet ever retaining clarity of contemplation.

In a word, we don't make out Masha or Richard II by behaving well, by maintaining decorum, by not sneezing or wandering in the aisles, or by relaxing in our limply sensitive receiving souls. We create them with the actor, by a labor of constructive imagination—arduous, deep, testing. And just as there are good readings of poems, fine "audience work," so, in Péguy's words, there are excellent seeings of plays, harmonious, rhythmic representations on the stage of the mind, attendings as honest, clear, and innocent as a flower blossom or a peach.

Ah, says a voice, you claim this activity has been banished from tickle-touch theater? Certainly it hasn't much of a place there. Absorption, attentiveness, concentration on otherness— these are hard for a playgoer to sustain in a situation in which the immediate urgent question inside him is: Does that actor heading my way mean to hit (kiss, fondle, solicit) me? Security vanishes, and, with it, guarantees of continuous outward focus. It's not all loss, naturally. Challenge and interruption are values, when sparingly, pointedly used; they can awaken the mind to action. But are there not limits to this action? Could a man write a chapter of a novel amid the uncertainty thus aroused, amid such promptings to nervous self-regard? Yet the good playgoer is, for the length of *his* performance, like a novelist: he is an interpreter, a provider, filler-in, reader-creator of motives, an active, strenuous, comprehensive intelligence.

Ah, says another voice, how comes it that an occupation so noble no longer turns people on? —You could say in answer that the trouble stems from the virus, Skepticism; people hate thinking of themselves as illusion-prone, connable by playactors. Or you could say the trouble is that people reared in a cave of self-hyphenation (self-this, self-that, self-realization, self-encounter, self-involvement, etc.) can't bear the prospect of self-diminution, and despise the notion of laboring over any character not their own. Or you could speak flatly of imaginative incompetence: in ages when men knew each other, when turpitude and virtue took the form of visible, trackable, right-or-wrong relations between one man and his neighbor, people were sharp at fathoming each other. Now they're clumsier, and embarrassed at their clumsiness.

But all this chatter scarcely fits the situation. What was wanted there by the punch bowl was just a way to say—lightly, quickly, provocatively—that, Yes, sure, it's wonderful to like something. Lovely to hear the Becks praised. But . . . It's not quite true that in Olden Times, before this Revelation, audiences "just sat there," locked up, locked in, mere blobs. I remember (for the record, "I" is a mid-fortyish lad) being loose-limbed and easy in a theater not on demand but in delight. I remember a disciplined freedom that nevertheless seemed every instant limitless. I remember whole hours in which, through constant steady inventings and piecings-out at once decorous and wild, I and neighbors roundabout were becoming—uninterruptedly becoming, for only our imaginations touched—everything *we* wanted to be. . . .

America the Unimagining

A man in his early fifties, vigorous, strong-faced, well liked in his town; family man, business success (small-city merchandising operation). No reader but a great keeper-up—business papers, hard news, world events, facts that matter. Pleasures? He "gets a kick out of" gadgets and machines—wild stereo layout in the cathedral living room, complicated ship-to-shore gear on his boat, a genuine systems approach for stock control in the stores. Further pleasures: he's outdoorsy, handy at home, a Dartmouth man, skier, active in business and community clubs, nonchurchgoer, nonpolitical argufier. . . .

At parties he doesn't talk much to women. Also, he stands back a little from his kids. Pleasant-tentative with his bright daughter, straight-arrowish "Dad" with his teen-aged boys. Stands back, too, from the "creative" phases of the business—buying, advertising, display, and so on—leaving this to a younger brother. (Let something "real sticky" turn up anywhere, though, and nobody but himself can cope. Who else, for instance, would be up to a face-off with the old family friend, one of his store managers, when the detective service reports the man is robbing them blind?) As for a personality profile:

"I am more interested in a man's behavior than in his inner life." Check. "In shaping character, externals are more important than inner tendencies." Check. "I sometimes have trouble figuring out the behavior of people who are emotionally unstable." Check. "Math is one of my best subjects." Check. "I think I'm practical and efficient when there's something that has to be done." Check. "I don't have the temperament for the 'romantic' point of view." Check. "I have few emotional problems." Check. "A first principle with me is that it's a man's duty to adjust himself to his environment." Check. "I am a fairly conventional person." Check. "My relations with other people are usually uncomplicated." Check. "My ideas are more often sound and sensible than unusual or imaginative." Check. "I say what I have to say in a few simple words so that I'm easily understood." Check. "There's a lot in the economic interpretation of history." Check. "I find it easier to deal with concrete facts in one special field than with general ideas about man or nature." Check. "I think science offers as good a guide as any to the future." Check. "When I'm working out a problem I try to stick as close as possible to the facts." Check. "I enjoy an intimate conversation with one person more than general conversation with several." No. "When I hear a person talk, I think more about his personality than I do about what he's saying." No. "I think I have a good understanding of women." No. "I love to talk about my innermost feelings to a sympathetic friend." Nah. "I often think I can feel my way into the innermost being of another person." No. "It takes a good deal to make me angry." Check. "Unselfishness and sympathy are more desirable than high ideals and ambitions." False. "I'm apt to make up stories by myself about the private thoughts and experiences of the people I meet." No. "I believe the world may be well lost for love." No. "I live in my imagination as much as I do in the external world." No. "I dislike everything that has to do with money—buying, selling, bargaining." Oh, sure. "I like being in the thick of the action." Yes, emphatically. "I like to have people about me most of the time." Yes, emphatically. . . .

Other items (not on the Harvard clinic test) worth noting about this man? One: Inclined to treat characters as functions, he regularly "explains" people by telling you what they do (a parenthetical phrase—Harry's a doctor, Hank's a cop, Lucille's had a pair of twins). Another point: The fellow is good to tie up by on a sloppy night at Southwest Harbor, and makes, in general, a fine summer neighbor—fun outings to the island, family picnics, softball on the sand, sun's over the yardarm, and so on. Further point: When you step away from him, sit in judgment, dwell on his limits, you feel like a heel. You discover again that one of the several reasons for not judging is that the minute it's done, the judge is judged, stands fully visible in his own fatuity and self-congratulation, beyond sympathy, ripe for sentence himself. Yet another item: The man "beheld" is representative. Tens of millions are excluded from his place, just at this moment; going up from the middle in society is where you're likely to find him, not from the middle down. But the excluded millions can't forever escape; even now they are being graded "up" on his curve. Every year the movement of economic life shoots tens of thousands toward him—into his set of mind, his style, his inward truth. He is no "middle-class stereotype," in short: he is an American destination or finish line, the possible end of the race.

Finally, last point about the man: He is in trouble. There's a withering in him, a metaphorical arm gone, some limb, some key part missing, something stunted or ungrown. The present judge speaks quickly, on the run, hoping to hide himself from the next judge: The man just described is, in one flat word, *unfulfilled*.

To say as much is, by instant extension, to discount the seriousness of the famous American commitment to the ideal of individual self-fulfillment. And while such discounting is standard practice among the knowing, it isn't at first glance easy to defend. Granted, the language in which national commitments and values are usually spelled out—the language of civics classes and Scouting Award nights—does beg to be mocked. "The social organization of America is compatible with its free political institutions. . . . America is a society in which equality of opportunity is supported by specific social mechanisms, including classlessness, a wide spectrum of inviolable and equal individual rights guaranteed to all individuals, guarantees of minimum welfare for all and special assistance to any that are at unusual economic disadvantage. . . . Enhancing the dignity of the individual citizen, developing his capabilities for self-fulfillment, is a prime concern of the American government. . . . The environments which help to shape the character of the individual—his home life, education, religious training, occupation, etc.—are in varying degrees matters of public concern. The object of this concern is to develop typical traits of character—independence of spirit, respect for the rights of others, cooperativeness, sense of civic responsibility—and others which will make the individual a better, more constructive citizen." Formulations like these cry out for qualification, amendment, hints of stylish self-restraint. Some humility, please.

But the cry for humility can itself become cant. Spells of living abroad in middle-class communities—leafy Edgbaston in England, say, or a Costa village in Portugal—offer only ambiguous testimony on the matter of the American versus European sense of civic responsibility. But in the area of attitudes and policies concerning education, those ambiguities disappear. The cause of "trained excellence" is Everyman's cause in America; my right to as much education as I can bear goes relatively unchallenged. No events, no crisis, seemingly, can interrupt the national dream of self-realization through mental strife. And no taxpayer protest ever badly smutches this piety. Two years ago, after the peace demonstration at the Pentagon, President Johnson, meeting with a group of teachers at the White House, turned eloquent—some might have said moving—on the subject of self-realization and the school. Appointments this morning, he explained, with the National Security Council and with the President of Mexico—but you, you teachers, you're more important. Whatever else they said about him, the President went on, they would have to say that because of programs he instituted, a million people were in college this year who would not otherwise have had a chance to go. And how much more remained to be done! Four men out of ten on earth could not read or write! He himself was returning to teaching when his political career was over.

The books on the Cabinet Room shelf suggested an absence of

a passion for the higher literary culture—O. Henry, a high school
physics text, a high school chemistry text, and the like. (There
has been no report that President Nixon has replaced them.) The
few educational institutions in the country where the idea of
standards is well rooted are meritocratic in assumption—which
means not only antiaristocratic but antidemocratic as well. By far
the larger part of the huge federal expenditures in the field of
education supports phases of the defense program. And, more
important than any of this, profound inequities still exist in the
American system of public education. But from none of this does
it follow that the cause or dream in question was a sham. The old
programs and the new—Head Start, the regional educational
laboratories, the tuition loan bank—have flaws, cannot meet
every need. But the motive behind them is, in essence, no more
suspect than the motive behind the foundation of the first free
public education system on earth. That motive is the nurture of a
citizen useful to the community at large but also decently
developed for himself—gifts realized, mind awake, wholeness
intact. An unmockable aim, in sum: dignity for man.

And yet, and yet: the Product of It All looks out from the
mirror and reveals himself to be—stunted. Somewhere—not simply in the stereotype of himself but in his actuality—he is locked
in himself; somewhere he is fixed in an inhuman rigidity; somewhere there is a "malfunction." How to account for this? Has the
nation from the start been the captive of theories about the
formation and nurture of individual selfhood that are wrong-
headed—theories that are obstacles in themselves to self-realization? Is there a uniquely American muddle about fulfillment? If
so, what is its nature? How is it to be solved?

Stupidity alone answers confidently—but several relevant observations come to mind. Chief among them is that, for complex
social, historical, and cultural reasons, the nature of human
growth—in particular, the central role of the imagination in
determining its rate and quality—has not often been placed
clearly before the national view.

Commentators by the hundreds score the country off for garishness, gross materialism, unspirituality; few focus on the poverty of its conception of personal growth. Yet that is the fairer target. The nation prates of self-realization, and rests in near obliviousness that my humanness depends upon my capacity and my desire to make real to myself the inward life, the subjective reality, of the lives that are lived beyond me. The nation feeds itself on rhetoric about "individual rates of progress"—and yet possesses little knowledge, if any, of the steps by which the human being becomes itself, the separate, private acts of the imagination on which the achievement of personhood depends.

And, to repeat, this ignorance or obliviousness is no mystery. Human growth stems from the exercise of our power to grasp another being's difference from within. How can that truism maintain itself among a people convinced of the fundamental sameness of men? As Tocqueville long ago pointed out, the myth of sameness is a keystone in the deep structure of American belief. (Tocqueville's specific point was that the American protest on behalf of "the individual" was rooted in the assumption that all individuals, once free "to be themselves," would desire the same things and feel in the same ways.) And it is a fact that the moral imperative of the imaginative act is rarely proclaimed in American public or cultural life. A Negro singer invited to a White House conference bursts out in condemnation of the guests for the unreality of their proposals, their abstractness when seen in the light of her experience. The First Lady's eyes moisten. Shaken but proud she responds that she "cannot understand" the outburst; she has not had the same experience. And in the morning the country's best newspaper, *The New York Times*, editorially salutes the First Lady for her "candor," agrees that the feelings and sense of life of the black community are beyond our imagining, and consigns all whites to blank, useless, uncomprehending pity.

And the story is not different on the contemporary intellectual scene. It is a French voice—Jean-Paul Sartre's—not an American voice, that is heard urging men to more intelligent conceptions of human growth, demanding that they break free of the notion that others have no life except that which they exhibit when serving as the material out of which we fashion our experience. (". . . there are men who die without—save for brief and terrifying flashes of illumination—ever having suspected what the *Other* is. The horizons of my life are infinitely shrunk.") And among recent philosophers it is a German voice—Max Scheler's—not that of an American, which dares to formulate an equation setting out relations of identity between individual growth, the perfection of love, and a grasp of the full distinctness and separateness of another human being. ("Love calls explicitly for an understanding entry into the individuality of *another* person *distinct in character* from the entering self . . . a warm and wholehearted endorsement of 'his' reality as an individual, and 'his' being what he is. . . . In love . . . there is built up, within the phenomenon itself, a clear-cut consciousness of two *distinct* persons. This consciousness is not merely a starting point; it reaches full maturity only as love pursues its course.")

What is more, a backward glance at the American cultural heritage confirms that the most powerful voices of American literary culture have been precisely those which, in one manner or another, have been most committedly hostile to the enterprise of attentive imaginative concentration on the fathoming of individual differences. D. H. Lawrence, in his *Studies*, broods hard on the stunted quality of the selves created in the writing of Poe and Whitman, and attributes it in the end to their incapacity to imagine and value a *separate* otherness. Love was a theme for both, but for neither was it a possibility; each man was drawn by fantasies of merging, total engrossment, loss of awareness of the other as separate—fantasies that teased him into confusing "understanding" with the act of sinking one's soul in another.*
And wherever the engrosser or merger disappears from American letters, an even more frightening figure—the self-bound man (Captain Ahab is the Prince)—stands forth in his place. In

* A version of this now turns up in Love Generation mystic-union gabble (You-am-I and I-am-you, etc.).

Emerson, for example, self-fulfillment appears to require an absolute denial of others, a massive, unrelenting independence, a readiness for isolation. Responding to a culture of conformity, this sage declared that a man bent on realizing himself must learn to carry himself in separation from otherness—"as if everything were titular and ephemeral but he." Widen the gulf, Emerson cries:

> We must go alone. I like the silent church before the service begins, better than any preaching. How far off, how cool, how chaste the persons look, begirt each with a precinct or sanctuary! So let us always sit.

Or again:

> At times the whole world seems to be in conspiracy to importune you with emphatic trifles. Friend, client, child, sickness, fear, want, charity, all knock at once at thy closet door, and say, "Come out unto us." But keep thy state; come not unto their confusion.

Or yet again:

> Live no longer to the expectation of these deceived and deceiving people with whom we converse. Say to them, O father, O mother, O wife, O brother, O friend, I have lived with you after appearances hitherto. Henceforward I am the truth's. . . . If you are noble, I will love you; if you are not, I will not hurt you and myself by hypocritical attention.

Emerson does allow that he could love another, if the person were noble; and every Emersonian knows how risky it is to fix the man in a single attitude. But separateness, far more often than involvement, is the theme that rouses him to lyricism; the poetry in him inclines strongly to the view, saying it once more, that becoming a fulfilled man means drawing oneself more tightly, consciously, firmly back within the limits of the primal existent self.

And that view or stance turns up repeatedly in American literature, in popular culture (the art Western), everywhere in American society. (It may even whisper to us in the writings of David

Riesman and Nathan Glazer; the utopian archetype of self-realized man described by them as "autonomous" has a definite taste for Emersonian gestures against otherness.) Over and over we are enjoined to find "our own thing," "our own bag," in the hippie phrase. And again and again the success of our search is presumed to depend upon our power to cut ourselves off, to harden the wall around us, not only to march to the beat of our own drum, but seemingly to hear no other sound.

There are, of course, countervoices here and there. Though his message did not cut through, smothered in clichés of life adjustment, John Dewey frequently dwelt on connections between human growth and sound education of the imagination—that instrument by which people gain in "flexibility, in scope, and in sympathy, till the life which the individual lives is informed with the life of nature and society." More than one American research psychologist has convinced himself of the centrality of imagination in the course of human development, and has attempted inquiries into the nurture of the imaginative man—witness the labors of Henry Murray and his associates at Harvard in the late 1930's. "Self-Other" theories of growth, which stress self-dramatization and imaginative role-playing, have a place in the history of American philosophy, owing chiefly to the writings of George Herbert Mead. ("The self by its reflexive form announces itself as a conscious organism which is what it is only so far as it can pass from its own system into those of others, and can thus, in passing, occupy both its own system and that into which it is passing. . . . Shut up within his own world . . . he would have no entrance into possibilities other than those which his own organized act involved. . . . It is here that mental life arises.")

And there is one great, seldom-studied American who put the case for fulfillment as dependent upon imaginative growth in utterly unambiguous terms—I speak of Charles Horton Cooley, a founder of American sociology. In *Human Nature and the Social Order* (1929), Cooley laid it down that:

> . . . the imaginations which people have of one another are the *solid facts* of society. . . . I do not mean merely that society must

be studied *by* the imagination—that is true of all investigations in their higher reaches—but that the *object* of study is primarily an imaginative idea or group of ideas in the mind, that we have to imagine imaginations. The intimate grasp of any social fact will be found to require that we divine what men think of one another. Charity, for instance, is not understood without imagining what ideas the giver and recipient have of each other; to grasp homicide we must, for one thing, conceive how the offender thinks of his victim and of the administrators of the law; the relation between the employing and hand-laboring classes is first of all a matter of personal attitude which we must apprehend by sympathy with both, and so on. . . .

Nor did Cooley stop here—with a mere definition of an appropriate area of inquiry for his field. He went on to assert that the quality of imaginative sympathies is the surest measure of the degree of human growth and fulfillment:

One's range of sympathy is a measure of his personality, indicating how much or how little of a man he is.

And he was certain beyond doubt that those who deprecated this sympathy, shrugged it off with prattle about *sensitivity*, missed its richly complicated nature and meaning:

[Sympathy] is in no way a special faculty but a function of the whole mind to which every special faculty contributes, so that what a person is and what he can understand or enter into through the life of others are very much the same thing. We often hear people described as sympathetic who have little mental power, but are of a sensitive, impressionable, quickly responsive type of mind. The sympathy of such a mind always has some defect corresponding to its lack of character and of constructive force. A strong, deep understanding of other people implies mental energy and stability; it is a work of persistent, cumulative imagination. . . .

But if there is a native tradition which understands the nurture of the imagination to be a key to general human growth, it is, by all odds, a minority tradition, far away from the center of popular belief. The weight of the general culture presses continually toward feats of objectification—objectification of labor (the assembly line, time study), of love (sex research), of desire (image-making, consumer research). At the center stands the conviction that fulfillment is deliverance into a function—a job, a title, a carpet, an income, a pool, somebody else's respect. I, the free American, am free to "find my own place," my "social niche," my "professional slot." I go forth from myself, I *go places,* ranch house to White House, dropout to Ph.D., twelve dollars weekly to a hundred dollars a day. And up the line, where I have it made: I "am more interested in a man's behavior than in his inner life"; I believe man's first duty is to "adjust himself to his environment"; I doubt that anyone can "feel his way into the innermost being of another person"; I don't seek inward truths. . . .

Is mockery in order? The objectifying American culture can be damned for having only once in its history concerned itself intensely with the matter of precisely what this or that individual man felt in this or that instant of time (the occasion was the period of witch trials in the seventeenth century, where it was found useful to know the inward workings of the devil). It can be damned as well for having consistently refused to introduce into its elementary educational system those "studies"—improvisation, mime, dance, dramatics—that elsewhere in the West are accepted as the basic human efforts at developing an imagination of otherness. It can be damned, more fiercely, for its incalculable failures of imagination—for example, its incapacity to make real to itself the inward life, man by man, woman by woman, child by child, of its black people.

But there are, here as always in life, qualifications to be entered: If there is no imagination of deprivation among us, there is at least guilt at good fortune, and this has sufficed to rebuild a world or feed a dozen famines. And in any event, it is not seemly for a professing humanist to lay down accusations here, for the American humanist—the teacher and scholar whose texts and knowledge should have been the greatest resources of those in pursuit of the truth of "the other subject"—has himself been a cop-out, an objectifier, a character madly eager to turn art itself into a "body of objective knowledge" to be "mastered" for "career examinations."

The point of substance, in fine, lies beyond accusations or "cultural critiques." It is a matter simply of a general, culture-wide dimming of the lights of inward life, a matter of failed encounters, missed meetings, hands that do not reach out, minds that hear the lock turn in their prison doors.

It is nighttime, the Maine harbor again. A lantern in the rain, motion of shore waters, a welcome, a beginning . . . But we don't go on, neither he nor she nor I. "My ideas are more often sound and sensible. . . ." "I say what I have to say in a few simple words. . . ." No hardrock, an occasional pot putterer, we would nevertheless prefer that people "not get ideas about us." And as for the famous still sad music of humanity, "we" don't hear it much. We don't flow; we hold on tight inside; we do the generous thing over and over, and invariably do it ungenerously; we see and feel and imagine ourselves to be highly responsible, competent, the solid people of the earth, the independents, the resilients, the unwhiners.

And for that idea or vision of self, some among us pay a lot—gouge out their innerness—become less than men.

Supergrow

At first glance they look downright insignificant—the kid fixers, the Supergrow brainfood crowd. Their product says what it is on the package, witness such hard-selling titles as these: *How to Double Your Child's Grades in School, How to Raise a Brighter Child, Give Your Child a Superior Mind, College Begins at Two*, etc. None of the authors is famous. (The big sellers are Eugene M. Schwartz, Isabelle P. Buckley, Siegfried and Therese Engelmann, and Joan Beck.) None holds a top establishment job. (Mrs. Beck's perch is the Chicago *Trib*, Schwartz is "in" Executive Training Techniques, Mrs. Buckley taught school in Hollywood and has some stars for fans, and Mr. and Mrs. Engelmann, the comers of the lot, fill a "research associates" slot in education at a making-it midwestern state U.) And as for the group's moral as opposed to pedagogical assumptions, they're as old as the Protestant Ethic—no ties with tricky New Thought—and rouse smiles as well as pain.

Humor doesn't, to be sure, get a conscious play in Supergrow books. A typical page of this writing—see Mrs. Buckley's *College Begins at Two*—quotes J. Edgar Hoover as a "spiritual authority," plumps, stiff-lipped, for a school-as-war metaphor ("the more disciplined the troops the fewer the casualties"), and cries up infant heroes like "Peter," whose "first college courses commenced" when he was two ("No wonder he was an enthusiastic little boy, for he knew where he was going")—all without a trace of a grin.

But here as elsewhere the straighter the face, the funnier the turn. Supergrow texts often favor sock-it-to-'em chapter heads ("How to Power Read," "How to Burn Facts into Your Mind"), and other belt-em and butt-em ploys:

> Teach [your child] to read aggressively. Actively. Tearing the ideas out of the pages with the techniques we are showing him in this book. [Schwartz, *How to Double Your Child's Grades*]

They print pinpoint schedules of development suitable for nurseries in sci-fi-flicks:

> By the time the child is 34 months old, he should know his capital letters perfectly. . . . The child should learn to count to ten by the time he is 30 months. . . . By the time the child is 3, he should know all the position words. . . . Point at these [geometric] shapes when the child is 28 months old. . . . [Engelmann and Engelmann, *Give Your Child a Superior Mind*]

They offer countless "Shut up, he explained" situations:

> Go over the [planet] chart at least once a week, beginning when the child is about 3 and ¾. Tell him what these balls on the chart are. "These are the planets in the solar system." Then explain what that means. [Engelmann and Engelmann, *A Superior Mind*]

And everywhere in their pages you run into the playpen polymaths of the future, characters it'll be criminal to deprive of the vote:

> Before the child enters kindergarten he can learn the basic rules of language, learn the alphabet, learn the names of the geometric shapes and begin counting, learn to spell, tell time, add, subtract, multiply, divide, understand fractions and basic algebra, learn to read, learn to deal with such complex mathematical problems as the squares of numbers, equations, factors and exponents. . . . [*A Superior Mind*]

Many a Supergrow writer, furthermore, has a gift for barkcrcsc from which comic excesses regularly flow:

Let me be perfectly clear on this point. Your child's grades—if he applies these techniques—will actually double. If your child is graded by a percentage point system rather than letters, this doubling process will result in an improvement of about ten to fifteen points. . . . Where he had 70 before he may now reach 80. [Schwartz, *How to Double . . .*]

And some are given to fits of italics which, though seriously, even fiercely, intended, read like cartoon balloons. (*"It is too late!"* shrills Grandma Buckley at the parents of some kid let go till he was six. "You must *push him!*" shout the Engelmanns, banging their crop on a crib.)

There are, of course, bad moments—times when Supergrow edges off into pathos or mystery, moments when it's hard to work up a grin. These occur often in the miracle or testimonial parts of the books, wherein one or another hurt baby held ineducable is hustled grimly into the joys of the mind:

In Florida, a fragile, dark-haired girl of forty-five months was reading a third-grade book to her father, a surgeon. Severely brain-damaged from birth and still unable to sit up or walk, Debbie had repeatedly been diagnosed as mentally retarded. At two well-known medical centers, her father had been advised to place her in an institution as a "human vegetable." Yet now, although she was not yet four, Debbie had a reading vocabulary that exceeded 1000 words. [Joan Beck, *How to Raise a Brighter Child*]

And abrupt changes of subject tend to bring on grossness, as when the Supergrow writer interrupts a math lesson for a chat on charm:

Help the child to develop desirable personality characteristics. Harold charges into the kitchen. "I want a cookie," he announces. "Sorry," his mother says, "that's not the way to ask for it." "Please!" Harold says. "No, not in that tone of voice." Harold flashes a frozen grin. "May I please have a cookie?" She hands him a cookie. "I can do a trick," he says. He motions for her to bend over. Then he hugs her and kisses her on the cheek. She gives him another cookie, and he runs outside.

Harold's mother has a rule: only one cookie in the afternoon. But this rule is not like the one about taking a nap or crossing the street. This rule is made to be broken. Harold's mother uses it to encourage Harold to develop desirable personality characteristics. She is showing him that *some* rules (and only *some*) can be broken with "charm." [*A Superior Mind*]

But despite the grossness, and the comedy, and the apparent general mockableness of kid-fixing in the large, Supergrow does possess cultural interest. Its testimony isn't unique in all areas, admittedly. Head Start, the revitalized Montessori movement, Omar Moore and his Responsive Environment Machine, the Carl Bereiter projects at the Illinois Institute for Research on Exceptional Children, and many other developments testify to the impact, on popular and professional minds, of the so-called revolution in theories of early childhood learning—that high-fashion, possibly unwholesome blend of Bruner and Piaget now on every lip. Supergrow texts add but a footnote to this evidence. And since teacher-critics like Herndon, Holt, Kozol, and Kohl, and writers like Goodman, Leonard, and Friedenberg have already richly documented the charge that America is too preoccupied with "cognitive learning," the new evidence implicit in Supergrow—no place in these books for the "affective"—is more or less *déjà vu*.

On other themes, though, Supergrow provides fresh perspectives. On the matter, for instance, of contemporary Horatio Algerism, or the bootstrap myth. The Supergrow audience is, as would go without saying, concerned about upward mobility. And at its coarsest and grubbiest—the work of Eugene M. Schwartz—Supergrow exploits the concern directly, pressing the connection between college degrees and lifetime earnings, stimulating anxieties about "falling behind," speaking in traditional Algerist idiom.

But elsewhere subtle new mutants appear. In Mrs. Beck's *How to Raise a Brighter Child* there are signs that some American Algerists are currently in the market for masks. The ideal reader of Mrs. Beck's book has a lot in common with the old-style Dad-on-the-make-for-his-kid; he's a worrier, his competitive nerves are a-jangle, he's tormented about his boy's prospects of getting ahead. Yet when this man worries, he's ashamed of it, and eager to ease the shame, and Mrs. Beck helps him ingeniously. She takes up a carefully judged position about overambitiousness that lets him confront his pushiness—and dissociate himself from it:

> Early learning doesn't mean that you should try to teach your three year old to read or make him a status symbol, or because your neighbor's child can read, or because you want to be sure he gets into Harvard fifteen years from now. You aren't trying to make a six year old out of a four year old, or turn a nursery school into a first grade, or deprive your moppet of the chance to be a child.

And after thus showing him who he isn't, she shows her reader who he is—a chap interested in home-teaching not for the sake of the rat race, but because at bottom he's a "pure science" type, an explorer, a voyager, a taster of life's joys:

> Early learning does mean that you try to understand your youngster's innate drive to learn, to explore, to fill his developing brain's urgent needs for sensory stimuli and satisfying learning experiences, just as you try to understand and fill the needs of his body for nourishing foods. You aren't stuffing his brain with facts so he'll make Phi Beta Kappa, any more than you give him vitamins to force his growth so he'll make the Chicago Bears' backfield. . . .

The easy-rider stance adds gentility to trad Algerist competitiveness and envy. And while the result may not qualify as moral progress—except in the eyes of cynics who associate moral progress with higher hypocrisies—it does constitute (at the minimum) a tonal break with the past.

And the same can be said, for different reasons, about another style of Algerism found in Supergrow texts—most notably in the Engelmanns' *Give Your Child a Superior Mind*. On its face *Superior Mind* is a work of standard design. The package contains strategies for teaching a child to tell time, point at an object, creep up on concepts—fast-slow, tall-short, and the like. And the promises made are of normal extravagance. (The authors claim to have a surefire method of teaching reading, "a program with the confusion, doubt, and uncertainty removed.")

But the Engelmanns address a reader who, no less distant from the Algerist norm that Mrs. Beck's reader, is nevertheless significantly different from hers. The Engelmanns' reader has no social pretensions, no need for masks—is in fact a reluctant Algerist at best. He's a doubter, a cynic, a disbeliever in the gospel of Work-Your-Way-Up, a person whose prime problem as a teacher would be defeatism born of a conviction that the child he's teaching isn't fated to learn. This defeatism belongs, speaking bluntly, to the ghetto, and the Engelmanns deal with it in the same curt, authoritarian way that they deal with most other attitudes and subjects. (People who have watched Mr. Engelmann at work in a classroom with young children say he puts his pupils "through the wringer"; his writings indicate he would regard that account of him as praise. See Maya Pines, *Revolution in Learning, The Years from Three to Six*, Chapter 4.)

Still, these authors do deal with defeatism. They know other people exist besides university lab-school parents, spawners of suburban SAT sharks. (Siegfried Engelmann collaborated with Carl Bereiter three years ago on a book called *Teaching Disadvantaged Children in the Preschool*. The hard-driving, skill-centered Bereiter-Engelmann methods are now being tried out on five thousand students in twelve American school systems. The systems are among eighty participating in Follow Through, a program for first-graders who've been through Head Start; Ocean Hill-Brownsville is among them.) And the principle aim of their effort appears to be to seed belief in upward mobility in just the areas wherein pessimism and self-hatred have for decades smothered it. Again and again the Engelmanns hammer at their doctrine: Nobody is beyond help; moment-to-moment encouragement and unremitting reenforcement must be the rule; every child can earn a chance to rise. Again and again a swift registering eye focuses on the damage done by parental or teacherly negativism and despondence:

> A trained observer can quickly spot a child who has been led to believe that he is stupid. The child will manage to give the wrong

response even if the task is relatively easy for him. When he is asked a question he tenses up because he *knows* what is going to happen. He knows that the wrong answer will slip out, and that he won't be able to hold it back. He pauses and his eyes dart. He fights down several words; then he says the wrong answer and he seems almost relieved. "I don't know that," he says. "I keep forgetting."

And, as indicated, the interest of the focus is that, like Mrs. Beck's, it marks a movement of cultural feeling. Mrs. Beck's book hints that, at social levels where overambitiousness was invariably self-righteous, self-criticism has begun to appear; the Engelmanns' book suggests that, at levels where defeatism was once too deep to know itself, there's now hope of stimulating consciousness of defeatism's destructive ways. On the one hand determined energy is bent on striking sparks of ambition, pricking the competitive nerve; on the other, it attempts to refine or subtleize the overambitious. And the contrasting efforts are an index—not a wholly depressing one, at that—of the mixed character of the present cultural hour.

Nor is Supergrow relevant only to Algerism and ambition. It has bearings on themes as large as that of Individualism and the Family. The emergence of the latter theme in history is—digressing a moment, for a purpose—a complex tale. The central strand, according to Philippe Ariès, was an achievement of privacy centuries in the making. And the achievement was bought at a price: forms of connectedness preceding the sealed-off private family vanished from the West. (No more open communication among generations and classes; an end to broad-scale human solidarity arising out of Everyman's solid knowledge of his betters and inferiors.) But in the exchange middle-class society gained the right to create a space for uniqueness for each new being brought to birth. The business of life became that of nourishing, within private walls, a sense of self, of difference, of special identity. No human unit was freer than the nuclear family to encourage the growth of separate egos; none better placed to sustain self-absorption or to keep off The Others—the endless parade of elders, rulers, owners, coworkers, the crowd that once allowed nobody a room of his own. ("All freedom," wrote Lord

Acton, "consists *in radice* in the preservation of an inner sphere exempt from state power.") And, in public rhetoric, the nuclear family continues to savor this freedom.

Maintaining it intact, however, has lately grown more difficult. Standardized food, clothing, and shelter, standardized working conditions, standardized public education and entertainment— these and other features of modern industrial civilization narrow the distance between the crowd world and the world of the private individual (the separate household, the sanctuary). As that distance narrows, the sense of family separateness and personal uniqueness weakens, and the family's ability to perform its newish function of developing significant differences among its members declines.

It's questionable, perhaps, whether that ability ever was equal to the task. The nuclear family as an institution may not have been capable, in the best of circumstances, of discharging the obligations laid on it by a culture of Individualism and Self-Realization. Nurturing separate wholenesses, ordering family life in a fashion that creates manageable distances between children and adults and among siblings, is, as every grown-up knows, a demanding job. Parent and child compete for space, are disposed to exact total capitulation from each other, and forget that, while safe separateness, serene private being, are the goals, the entire family seeks them, and none can be satisfied save through compromise, sacrifice, endless, amusing, exacerbating tradings-off.

Furthermore, the complexity and delicacy of the pursuit, sel-dom fairly rendered by artists or by social scientists, are often denied outright, opportunistically, in popular parents' manuals— see, most recently, Haim Ginott's *Between Parent and Child, New Solutions to Old Problems.** Everywhere in such texts the

---

* Dr. Ginott claims, plausibly, that children's separate being must be recognized and respected by parents, and that the only route toward genuine recognition lies through the imagination:

> The first step in the long-term program is a determination to become interested in what children are thinking and feeling inwardly, and not just in their outward compliance or rebellion. . . . All we need is an ear

language favored is that of "problems" and "solutions"; seldom is there an attempt to locate growing points for private egos. Everywhere the friendly guides give assurances that the combination of objectification and sympathy necessary to functioning parents can be attained by formula; nowhere do they glance at the evidence proving these assurances false. Nor is this because the evidence is in short supply. Most grown-ups, to repeat, could contribute lavishly from their experience. Few can have found the task of helping individuality to breathe and occupy its own space less than arduous, frustrating, contradictory; many have run from it back into the authoritarian "role models" of their own or their grandparents' bad dreams.

Or else back into the simplicity of the classroom. The advent of Supergrow—returning to the point—is a sign of the lure of that flight, and, as such, it's a telling symptom of the vulnerability of family to "community." When parents take upon themselves responsibility for school learning, when they announce that their account of their child's strengths, weaknesses, feelings, correct temper, and occupation precisely jibes with that of the school, when in short they behave in a manner implying that the home is

---

to listen, an eye to behold, a heart to feel. Our inner motto is: Let me understand. Let me show that I understand. Let me show in words that do not automatically criticize or condemn.

But the purpose of this recognition appears throughout Ginott's book as that of cooling kids, mediating fights. And, still worse, the body of the work—here, incidentally, is the major reason for its enormous success—the body of the work aims to persuade parents that the task is easy, all I need is a "heart to feel" and a bag of "effective four-step sequences" like the following:

1. The parent recognizes the child's wish and puts it in simple words; "You wish you could go to the movies tonight."

2. He states clearly the limits on a specific act: "But the rule in our house is 'no movies on school nights.'"

3. He points out ways in which the wish can be at least partially fulfilled: "You may go to the movies on Friday or Saturday night."

4. He helps the child to express some of the resentment that is likely to arise when restrictions are imposed: "It is obvious that you don't like the rule." Etc. Etc.

but an adjunct of the school, yet another subtle erosion of the imagination of difference occurs. The child takes the cultural wind straight on his bow and hangs defenseless, unable to set courses of his own. He perceives that his father, when most intentionally concerned with him, is in fact a mere extension of school people who have no private involvement of feeling with him; he perceives, as his father runs through the drill of letters, number, planets, that the world "beyond" privacy is the one Real World; he perceives (or will at length perceive) that the serious acts of life, the challenges, the major uses of mind and imagination, occur out there, in stock, standard-brand, public situations, not within private walls. Astonishing indeed if such perceptions didn't induce a depressed sense of the possibility of a private individuality.

—From which it follows: *à bas* Supergrow?* You do not come out here, I think, if you've worked in ghetto classrooms, K-3, or for that matter in any setting where children kill time at assignments they can't do. The relevant sight is a row of children "doing" commercial seatwork, unable to read—sitting at a table, being "good," copying a word now and then into a blank, moving their pencils and their lips. "We had ——— to drink at Christmas." A little girl chews her eraser, and, dutiful and serious, fills in the first word from the word list: "We had *overcoat* to drink at Christmas." Next desk: "Do not *kitchen* at the party." . . . With this sight in mind, as I say, you don't instantly scoff at early-education schemes, at any prekindergarten step that creates alternatives to victimization and waste.

But it's one thing not to scoff, and another to endorse. Most days after teaching black classes in "my" project, an hour or so of story-talk, acting out, easy back-and-forth, laughter, inquiry, animation, I go over the District of Columbia line and teach white suburban children the same age. And there's something to

* That line is taken by Eda Le Shan in *The Conspiracy Against Childhood,* a ferocious assault on early learning by a writer who aligns herself with John Holt, and appears to have little feeling for the comparative chances of rich and poor to learn to work their minds.

the sentimental or pastoral—or self-hating—claim that teaching is a flatter occupation Over There—more wariness, less response, sadness in the lucky middle-class eyes. Everybody reads, everybody's bright, boffo SATs lie ahead. No commercial seatwork. Yet the impression persists that participatory energies are greater in the ghetto—more appetite, more ease with the idea of breathing.

And you have only to admit this for a moment to be lost in the famous quandaries, viz.: Don't bug the kids: they breathe better if left alone. . . . Why should the "disadvantaged" recapitulate the experience of the middle class? What've they done to deserve that? —Ah, but rejecting the middle-class experience means denying the powerful awakening satisfactions of consecutive thought. —Ah, but embracing that experience means (sooner or later) declining into wanness, pallor, contempt for the very cause, Individuation, that nourished the middle-class rise. . . . Etc.

That the quandaries can't be straightened in a phrase doesn't signify that the only end of brooding about Supergrow—or about Supergrow vs. Innergrow—is ambiguity. For one thing, reading the books at hand does freshen the sense of the foolishness of pedagogical priorities fixed in ignorance of the areas of life (worlds of knowledge and feeling) over- and under-taught by the relevant nonschool environments. And, more important, it touches up belief in the notion that in some situations the young may need training in truancy as well as in application. "You teach your daughters the diameters of the planets," said Dr. Johnson, "and wonder when you have done that they do not delight in your company." And while it's wrong to press that button too hard—the great man isn't claiming that planets are boring, he's saying that parents shouldn't be—it's worse to wind the education dialectic (Supergrow vs. Innergrow) so tight that all the homely proportioning truths disappear.

We need to remember, that is to say, that we seek something more than proficiency or privacy or preparation for next year's objective tests. We want appetites and responsiveness, a feeling of personal unity and togetherness, belief in the possibility of meeting a problem by using the mind, openness to pleasures that can spring as easily from a "shocking" dirty word shared at age forty around the supper table, as from a thousand-word vocabulary picked up at three. We want a competency and self-reliance which, while not unrelated to manipulative skills, derive less directly from them than from the habit of inquiry into connections among visible bits of experience, keen practice at exploring "the working of each part on every part of the common life of men." We want children exhilarated by the onset of such competence and teachers absorbed in nurturing its increase. We want, in short, not doubled grades or "superior minds" or better "early education techniques," but a life-college good enough to begin at two. And if we miss the difference between the former and the latter, if we go on whoring after Supergrow slyness and Ivy SATs, like "realistic" deans of admission in the empty colleges of this day, we'll never make a start toward getting it.

How We Lost
the Sex Lab War

[1]

The world of mind divides itself, the halves berating each other in extravagances, competing destructively in situations that cry out for harmonious collaboration—where can a student find models of humane, wholistic concern?

The world of mind, building on foundations laid in the nineteenth century, develops detailed new knowledge with significance for the inward well-being of millions, and then allows reductionism, timidity, and vanity to deflect the passage of this knowledge to the public—how much can be said for contemporary intellectual life?

A story with bearings on these questions begins in 1954 with a decision of a young associate professor of obstetrics and gynecology at the Washington University Medical School to enter a field he'd been preparing for years: the laboratory study of human sexual response. The story ends with the announcement not many weeks ago by the same professor, Dr. William Masters, that the project's hugely publicized piece of equipment—a plastic artificial phallus—had been "disassembled," no plans in mind "for reconstruction." In the decade and a half between the decision and the disassembling, scores of sages, sexmongers, poets, and culture critics held forth in print on sex research, confusing issues or inventing them, distracting attention from significant realities of the subject. And, going at once to the matter of responsibility, the researchers themselves bore part of the blame, since they poured out a series of charges and simplistic rationales which obscured (and still obscure) the best uses and meanings of their undertaking.

The most tendentious of these charges was that the so-called literary or general-cultural view of human sex—every view, in short, that underemphasizes sex as physical activity pointed toward orgasmic release—is a lie that urgently requires scientific straightening out. The Washington University scientists didn't take this aggressive line publicly at the inception of their research; they took no line, for their chief concern at that time was to avoid a break in the voluntary press blackout which, as it developed, the St. Louis newspapers and wire services maintained about the sex lab into the sixties. But once they felt safe, they hit hard. Dr. Masters' earliest paper on sex research, a 1960 report appearing in the *Western Journal of Surgery,* lashed out at "literary fiction and fantasy" on the ground that it perpetuates an "unbelievable hodgepodge of conjecture and falsehood" in the area of sexual relations. The full-scale formal report of Masters' Reproductive Biology Research Foundation, brought forth in 1964 under the title *Human Sexual Response,* was presented, jaw out, as a compendium of "physiologic truth as opposed to cultural fiction." And even at the present late hour, the sex researchers are still pressing an attack, in interviews and essays, against bookish "traditionalists" whose chat about love and "mystery" foists (they say) "an incredible amount of misconception, fantasy and fallacy" upon people, nourishing "superstition and myth," weakening the sense of fact.

Predictably, literary types took unkindly to this abuse, and counterattacked even before publication of *Human Sexual Response.* A characteristic salvo was Leslie Farber's "I'm Sorry, Dear," printed in *Commentary* in 1964. Since the author was himself a psychiatrist and a former chairman of the Association of Existential Psychology and Psychiatry, the assault looked at first glance more internecine than two-cultural. The manner and matter of the piece, however, together with the circumstances of its publication, established that Farber spoke as a humanist. "I'm

Sorry, Dear" came decorated with a multitude of literary epi-
graphs and allusions (C. S. Lewis, Herman Melville, the Marquis
de Sade, Lionel Trilling, and Eleanor of Aquitaine figured in one
way or another). The essay opened, moreover, with a page of
invented dialogue, novelistically notated (the conversation of
lovers just following an unsatisfactory episode of lovemaking),
and was composed in a fashionable literary tone (stern, Sartrian,
sniffish).*

The minor charges in Farber's critique of Masters and Johnson
were that their sexology (1) made "both the brothel and pornography less exciting dwellings for our erotic investigation," (2)
removed the erotic life from "the traditional disciplines, such as
religion, philosophy, literature, which had always concerned
themselves with sex as human experience," (3) was overab-
sorbed with gadgetry "at the expense of any imaginative grasp of
the occasion" of love, and (4) was sick with democratic zeal
(Masters believes that "the more minute physiological developments [in lovemaking] should belong to every citizen," and he
increases "the political clamor for equal rights for women"). The
major charges were, first, that the new sexology had in effect
"invented" the orgasm as the essential part of woman's—and
man's—whole sexual experience (in olden days "the moment of
orgasm was not abstracted . . . and idealized," and was only an
"occasional" part of the experience); and, second, that the sexologists denied Original Sin, encouraged lovers "to will the
perfection on earth which cannot be willed," and thereby brought
upon men "the pathos which follows all such strivings toward
heaven on earth."

Important as the charges were, though, and frequent as their
reiteration soon became, neither Farber's nor any subsequent
literary response to the sexological crusade against "myth" was, in

---

* In explaining his belief that "sex for the most part has lost its viability
as a human experience," Farber cited modern man's self-conscious, willful
alienation from his own physicality, and rehearsed an argument about
knowing and being known through sex that was taken directly, without
acknowledgment, from Jean-Paul Sartre's *Being and Nothingness*.

a decisive sense, a matter of specific charges. The literary mind
built its case more through tone, nuance, implication, than
through discrete, answerable arguments. The impression con-
veyed was that sex research was merely an aspect of the decline
or collapse of Western culture. Farber and other littérateurs
adopted a voice of ironic resignation which spoke at every
moment—regardless of the ostensible subject—of the "inevitability" in a dying culture of an endless succession of corruptions.
They presented themselves as yearners for transcendence, people
with a fastidious, half-*spirituelle* distaste for physicality and
sensuality. And they constantly played off ideals and glories of
past (imaginary) worlds of love against the base actualities of
the modern sex research lab.

Farber himself concentrated on the central figures of Arthurian
romance (Queen Guinevere, Sir Galahad), and on the intense,
delicate doctrines of Courtly Love, in setting up the contrast.
Others ranged farther. The English poet and novelist David
Holbrook, for example, writing about "The Delusions of Sexul-
ogy" in the *Peace News*, invoked Duns Scotus, the medi-
eval philosopher who scorned "imperfect love . . . 'love of con-
cupiscence' . . . because it seeks the other for advantage." And
the American novelist George P. Elliott, for another, harked back,
in the *Hudson Review*, to heroic love affairs in Proust, reminding
his reader of the refinement of Swann's feelings "as the phrase
from Vinteuil's sonata is evoking tender memories of the days
when Odette was in love with him."

All, however, used these models of elegance, decorum, discipline, and superhuman grace from the cultural past for a similar
purpose, that of dramatizing the slobbishness of sex research
science. Think of Guinevere, think of Galahad, Farber told his
audience, and then think of people tasteless enough to welcome
the "prospect of arriving at the laboratory at 10:00 A.M., disrob-
ing, stretching out on the table and going to work in a somewhat
businesslike manner while being measured and photographed.
. . . (Thank you, Miss Brown, see you same time next week.)"
Think, said the novelist Elliott, think of marvelous Swann and

Odette, and then think of a "sane, taxpaying, tenured professor solemnly copulating with his wife on a cot in [the] laboratory, their arms strapped for blood-pressure readings, cathodes at their temples, cardio-tachographs zigging, their anuses wired, 'My bunny, my love, O sweetest joy!' Well, every man has the right to make himself look like a fool."

Imagine, said Holbrook, imagine the dignity and restraint of Scotus' mind engaged on its analysis of love, and then:

> Imagine . . . a group of scientists making the Masters-Johnson color film of a female masturbating: the faceless torso, the arm, the moving fingers, the erotic flush on the thighs, the moistening organ, the stiffening nipples, the physical contractions of orgasm, the fine film of sweat covering the whole body afterwards. Or imagine for that matter the group of overalled scientists observing dials, with a camera team working on a man and woman who have coition (having never met before) on the laboratory couch for a research fee. Sometimes the scientists stop them to make adjustments or measurements: then when they get going again the instruments are all set to time the physical features of orgasm: How often? How long? How many sperms? How acid or alkali? How strong is the ejaculation? Where did it go? Do the sperms survive?—Do the participants punch one another in their final ecstasy?

On both sides of the Atlantic dozens of other writers—panelists, reviewers of the Masters-Johnson volume, letters-to-the-editor men—echoed the literary complaint that a monstrous new vulgarity was poisoning the land.

As should be said, Masters and Johnson were not the only sexologists of the period who provided materials for abuse. The earlier, Kinsey or pollster school of research was still active in the mid-sixties, and produced several mockably formulaic statements of its findings—witness the following passage from a paper of a San Diego psychologist:

> Both men and women engage in the more serious types of sex play as the type of dating involvement increases. The men, however, are significantly more liberal in their actual conduct particularly for the

first few dates (NoK, N, PAWPBW, SI, $X^2 = 16.22$ 3df, p < 1 percent), frequent and continuous dating (NoK, N, PAWPBW, SI, $X^2 = 14.62$ 3df, p < 1 percent), and going steady (KN, PAW, PBW, SI, $X^2 = 15.62$, 3df, p < 1 percent) . . . [R. L. Karen, "Some Variables Affecting Sexual Attitudes, Behavior and Inconsistency." The paper included a key to symbols: N = nothing. K = kissing. PAW — petting above waist. PBW — petting below waist, etc.]

And as also should be said, there were occasions throughout the sixties when the ranks of literary antisexologists were swelled by writers who were cruder than the crudity they damned. The commonest offender was the novelist—a cluster of sex research novels appeared in the late sixties—and the reason for this was simple. Novels on the subject tsk-tsked and looked grave about the laboratory experiments, delivering short essays at key moments on lubricity, dehumanization, and such. Yet commercial exigency dictated that events inside the labs be depicted with seemly fullness, and this requirement set up counterstrains.

Consider, for instance, Robert Kyle's *Venus Examined* (1968). The implied argument of the book is that the ordinary stuff of life (and of novelese)—personal relations—cannot be kept out of the sex lab, despite the avowals and high intentions of the researchers. (In Kyle's sex lab, the volunteers fall in and out of love with each other, arrange secret meetings, seek to seduce their scientist-observers, etc. etc.) The overt argument—its spokesman is an English prof at Barnard who sits on the board of a foundation asked to fund the (electrical) phallus—echoes the standard charges:

> Your laboratory isn't the only place in the modern world where numbers have replaced names, where a machine is substituted for a living person, where action is separated from feeling and no act has any consequences. But somehow your modernity is a little more vivid! To me your copulation machine stands as a symbol of the other evil things that are being done to us in the name of science. It's too perfect! How skillfully it gives a woman her orgasmic relief, carrying

her out of the frustrations and compromises of ordinary life into a condition of perpetual spasm—

And the conclusion of the book is a wild passage of new Ludditeism that might have been—in the hands, say, of Nathanael West—a compelling bit of contemporary terror. (A discharged volunteer returns in bitterness to the sex lab, smashes the copulation machine, and is herself electrocuted in the act.)

But, to repeat, the various novelistic indictments of tastelessness, crudity, and vulgarity lacked force because of the density of vulgarity surrounding them in their own pages. In *Venus Examined* there are interminable discussions—not comically intended —about whether a lady who's *lost* her orgasmic capacity after participating in the project should sue the projectors. ("'You never had trouble having orgasms before, and we can prove that from Prescott's own records. . . . You could . . . sue him,' Anne said. . . . 'Would you turn down half a million bucks? They give that much for a leg.'") And a leering clumsiness marks nearly every episode of intercourse observed. (One gamey episode details the attempt of a Dr. Masters-type to teach a timid, previously "ineffective" husband named Hallinan to pleasure his lady via cunnilingus.)

Pots calling kettles black weren't the only factor adding to the confusion. A dozen conflicting unconscious attitudes and prejudices figured in the arguefying between sex scientist and littérateur from the start—elitism vs. egalitarianism, love of the past vs. optimism about the future, the sense of style vs. the relish of freedom, nostalgia for religious passion vs. delight in the "end" of superstition. And stock responses were everywhere the rule. The literary man told his audience that the scientist operated under the delusion that the isolatable, observable, physiological act was the "only" act of love—a delusion betraying irremediable inward coarseness. The scientist told his audience that if his idea of sex was limited, at least he believed sex existed. Nobody on his side ever claimed, he said, as the poet Holbrook claimed, that "there is really no such thing as sex." ("There is only," Holbrook added,

"the use of the sexual capacities of individuals to express potentialities of being.") Nor had anybody on his side ever denied, as
Farber denied, that sexual frustration was real. (Until recently,
Farber maintained, the unorgasmic woman had been "content
with the mystery and variety of her difference from man, and in
fact would not have had it otherwise.")

Inside the rhetorical exchanges, smothered, choking, there
were a few genuine and discussible differences of assumption
and value. But these were seldom in direct view. The antagonists
spoke as though convinced that the proper aim for each was the
complete discrediting, if not destruction, of the other. Not only
did they show small consciousness of the root causes of the furies
to which they were giving utterance; they appeared not even to
have considered asking the most pertinent question: What in this
instance will victory or defeat for either of us mean to everyone
else?

[2]

On both sides the root causes of the furies just mentioned are, of
course, various. Jealousy is in the equation, as well as snobbish-
ness, and resentment about lost eminence and power, and scorn
for private metaphor allowed to go public and pass itself off for
ages as truth. But there are other, less frequently noted items as
well. Not the least of these, on the literary side, is the humanist's
custom of abstracting science from general cultural history—
treating particular scientific enterprises as unique phenomena,
assuming that while this or that "controversial" experiment may
conceivably "belong" to some special field of science, such work
has no natural or logical place in the mainstream of liberal
humane inquiry. Again and again the assumption has proved
false, and the present episode is no exception. The case is that sex
lab research is a direct result (others are beyond counting) of a
long struggle waged by scientific *and* literary minds on behalf of
the Cause of intellectual inclusiveness—a struggle begun in the

nineteenth century, and still unfinished. Had the struggle not been waged, neither the Masters and Johnson investigation nor that of Kinsey over a decade ago could have been imagined, much less conducted. And both probes will probably soon impress more as markers of the progress of that Cause than for their particular findings.

To say this isn't to imply that Dr. Masters is a major intellect or that the cause of inclusiveness flourished because those who created it worked together in conscious coalition. Marx in the Manchester factories, Darwin gazing at a gang of Fijians, Frazer teasing out the meaning of the sacred grove at Nemi in *The Golden Bough,* Freud interpreting dreams and explaining displacement in the *Introductory Lectures on Psychoanalysis,* Lawrence creating Mellors in *Lady Chatterley's Lover*—these aren't thinkers in league. But a unity of effect can be felt in their work.*
The effect was to put men in touch with a range of material (behavior, values, symbolic acts, words, modes of feeling, thinking and perceiving) lying outside the official culture of the day—materials establishing that human reality, present or historic, wasn't fully represented in official images. And the demand for fuller representation has grown ever more insistent throughout this century. Comparative study of cultures and value systems, inquiry into the parallel evolution of man and animal, the development of psychoanalysis, new models of social and economic history, genetical research in the fields of art and literature—these and numberless other undertakings are directly traceable to the whetted appetite for news of the prefatory, disorderly, just possibly basic states of being which established culture ignored.

* A favored trick of the antisexologist was to deny this unity and dissociate literary men from the great changes of attitude and understanding brought about in the last century. Farber, for instance, claimed that literary artists who dealt with sex in their works thought of it in terms of "qualities such as modesty, privacy, reticence, abstinence, chastity, fidelity, shame." (Blake? Strindberg? Yeats?) Nowhere did he acknowledge that the accepted meanings of these terms have changed markedly in the last century and a half or that literary men were themselves responsible in large measure for the redefinitions.

—From which it follows that treating the original Masters and Johnson concept as a running down of intellectual energy, a symptom of contemporary irrationalism or decline of mind, is senseless. The project had honorable links with a dignified intellectual past, and, depending on the quality of its execution, it could have become an embodiment, minor but useful, of the best intellectual taste of the age. The current habit of culture is either to turn away from sexual intercourse, accounting it a private act, or to exploit it in public entertainment for commercial profit; both practices worsen social and moral problems, and contribute nothing to knowledge. Well enough, let us gaze straight at sexual intercourse, take it in as a definable, separable, natural phenomenon among phenomena—an act or event whose characteristics can be discerned, measured, and compared. And let us maintain that same perspective over the entire "field" of sexual behavior—masturbatory orgasms, homosexual experience, the experience of the prostitute, physiological response to pornography. Let us seek "truth of a sort," on the ground that it has value in itself, and has occasionally proved of use in encounters with "social problems."

Granted the Masters-Johnson project had comical as well as "shocking" aspects. The researchers shared the Yankee preoccupation with know-how; the passages in *Human Sexual Response* in which a personal voice (a hint of scoffing) cuts through the neutralism are usually those critical of false know-how:

> Most marriage manuals advocate the technique of finding the clitoris and remaining in direct manual contact with it during attempts to stimulate female sexual tensions. In direct manipulation of the clitoris there is a narrow margin between stimulation and irritation. If the unsuspecting male partner adheres strictly to marriage manual dictum, he is placed in a most disadvantageous position. He is attempting proficiency with a technique that most women reject during their own automanipulative experience.

Granted, too, Masters and Johnson, like many other scientists, exemplified the national relish of technological gimmickry; the culture of charcoal filters and poptops was perhaps reflected in the copulation machine:

> The artificial coital equipment was created by radiophysicists. The penises are plastic and were developed with the same optics as plate glass. Cold-light illumination allows observation and recording without distortion. The equipment can be adjusted for physical variations in size, weight, and vaginal development. The rate and depth of penile thrust is initiated and controlled completely by the responding individual. As tension elevates, rapidity and depth of thrust are increased voluntarily, paralleling subject demand. The equipment is powered electrically.

But America isn't through and through a joke, not even in the St. Louis project. There are some notable national elements in the research that only the most priggish literary aristocrat could take as ludicrous; they're especially vivid in the passages of *Human Sexual Response* recounting the life history and sexual experience of some participants in the project—passages that chronicle a movement from emptiness to light.

Consider the case of Subject D, a "34-year-old male, married 6 years and the father of two children." An only child, a minister's son, father now dead, mother a receptionist for a doctor. Profession: draftsman. College: two years. Reason for dropout: death of the father. "There is a history of strict parental control during the teenage years, and an excessive concern for social mores." No "automanipulative history" (meaning masturbation) until freshman year in college, and this single experimental episode was followed for a full year by a "severe guilt residual." Sophomore year an episode of petting leads once to "involuntary ejaculation, with the experience followed for several months by residual guilt feelings." Afterward for four or five years: prostitutes and masturbation, prostitutes and masturbation. Then Subject D marries. His bride is a business-school graduate. There is a record of relative failure in coition, though neither partner is lacking in desire. Years pass, the couple hears of the Masters and Johnson research; husband and wife make inquiry:

For orientation, five episodes were necessary after team interrogation. The first exposure was to background and equipment; during the second, coition was attempted without ejaculatory success. The third episode developed as successful coition for Subject D, but his wife was not orgasmic. During the fourth session both husband and wife were successful in individual automanipulative episodes, and in the fifth episode no difficulty was encountered by either partner in response to coital or manipulative stimuli. This pattern of freedom from restraint has been the rule in subsequent program exposure, much to the surprise of both husband and wife. The family has cooperated with long-range response-evaluation and male physiology programs. . . .

. . . Subject D was concerned with his own overcontrolled background, lack of sexual experience, and a considered degree of sexual response to coital or manipulative stimuli. This pattern of freedom incidence was reported as rare with coital exposure but consistent with manipulation. Subsequent to working in the program her orgasmic achievement during coition has risen to the 80 percent frequency level. She has not been multiorgasmic either during coition or automanipulation.

Subject D's wife has stated repeatedly that subsequent to program participation her husband has been infinitely more effective both in stimulating and in satisfying her sexual tensions. He in turn finds her sexually responsive without reservation. Her freedom and security of response are particularly pleasing to him. Together they maintain that they have gotten a great deal more out of cooperation with the program than they have contributed, and they wish to continue on a long-term basis.

The literary mind, the figure of style and breeding, may smile at such a recital, shaking his head at the cozy cure brought off with *Reader's Digest* ease—"The latest democratic dream: not guaranteed annual wages but guaranteed 'success' in bed." But the laughter is too easy. Everywhere in the West men and women by the millions burn, helplessly, within and without marriage, finger themselves off, torment themselves with guilt, belabor each other in silent, killing war—and that which helps them, that which lifts them momentarily beyond the meanness of their losing lives, can't really be despised. The Washington University study didn't aim at improving people's sex lives—but the directors knew that in a neutral setting homely words could be said that might effect change. A sense, in fact, of meanness conquered and ordinary life freshened here and there, surprised by joy, can be made out in the closing pages of the Masters and Johnson report by anyone as yet unfrozen in postures of *de haut en bas.* Doubtless connections exist between this new American fantasy—joyous sex for the masses—and others of the past: salvation through community colleges, salvation through Beethoven LPs. But there is dignity in the fantasy nevertheless, as in all humane egalitarianism, and beauty as well—the beauty of decency, generosity, and hope. With this in mind, and remembering the continuity of the project with intellectual tradition, the idea of abusing Masters and Johnson as sin and deviltry looks cheap.

[3]

But those who delivered the abuse *were* provoked to do so—which is to say that, when the full context of the sex lab war is studied, there's blame for everybody, not just for literary men. If the world of science has a right to be embarrassed for poets who miss the unity of rational inquiry in the immediate past, the world of letters has the right to be embarrassed in turn for scientists who persist in hawking superstitions of the kind implicit in Masters-Johnson chatter about "physiologic truth as opposed to cultural fiction." A major lesson of the sharpest contemporary thought, after all, stresses the mutuality of mythical and scientific understanding of "fact"; the pretense that "subjective" and "objective" realities can be crisply disentangled by any bright chap with a white coat, a stopwatch, and a mind unviolated by poetry is disingenuous if not dumb. Masters and Johnson learned that there is a sense in which coital and masturbatory orgasms, when compared in strict physiological terms, can be described as "the same." But the manner in which they reported this and a dozen other "challenges to myth" indicated that they had excluded attitudinal considerations, and were persuading themselves that the purely physiological man they posited wasn't a conceptual model, or abstraction, but a genuine human being. And the literary men who scored off this delusion did indeed have a point.

What is more, the sex researchers look to have been, on balance, a rather fearful lot. A striking portion of their evidence bore on the comparative intensity of male and female sexuality; the evidence suggested the edge belongs to the female. Yet the researchers never faced the findings directly: they trimmed in the presence of them or shyly turned aside. As might have been expected, fellow professionals called them out for their reticence. Writing in the *Journal of the American Psychoanalytic Association*, Dr. Mary J. Shurfey remarked, on the basis of the Masters-Johnson research, that "to all intents and purposes, *the human female is sexually insatiable in the presence of the highest degrees of sexual satiation*," and went on not only to draw attention to the possible social consequences of dissemination of findings in this area, but to chide the researchers for their evasiveness and self-censorship: *

* Dr. Shurfey commented first on the likeness between the sexual responsivity of the human female and that of certain higher primates: "having no cultural restrictions, these primate females will perform coitus from twenty to fifty times a day during the peak week of estrus, usually with several series of copulations in rapid succession. If necessary, they flirt, solicit, present, and stimulate the male in order to obtain successive coitions." After observing that "our myth of the female's relative asexuality is a biological absurdity," she noted that the satiation-in-insatiation state of the primate and human females parallels "the behavior ascribed to women during the prepatriarchal, Mesolithic period—and well into the Neolithic Bronze Age—of history. . . ." Her argument was that womankind's sexuality has been ruthlessly suppressed in the name of monogamy, and in service of a man-centered civilization. Since that suppression seems now to be easing ("a decided lifting of the ancient social injunctions against the free expression of female sexuality has occurred"), the present moment, Dr. Shurfey speculated, could well become one of cultural reorganization:

". . . one thing is certain: if women's sexual drive has not abated, and they prove incapable of controlling it, thereby jeopardizing family life and

The most provocative gesture of the sex researchers, however, wasn't finally a matter either of trimming or superstition. It was, instead, the rejection of imaginative flexibility—a gesture that smutched the very ideal of inclusiveness that brought the project to life. Brainy men can indeed stand to know everything, the nineteenth-century idealists had implicitly insisted. Not only can the full truth of human smallness, as well as of human nobility, be endured; it perhaps can be used for the betterment of this world. And those who use it, the argument ran, will become men of humor, blitheness, unarrogant skepticism. They will learn to take pleasure in their own deflation; they will become even-handed acceptors of the general human humiliation, steady riders, sound hearts. Thomas Mann spelled out the vision once in a famous address on "Freud and the Future," claiming that with the analytic revelation "a blithe skepticism has come into the world, a mistrust that unmasks all schemes and subterfuges of our own souls. Once roused and on the alert, it cannot be put to sleep again. It infiltrates life, undermines its raw naivete, takes from it the strain of its own ignorance . . . inculcates the taste for understatement . . . for the deflated rather than for the inflated words, for the cult which exerts its influence by modera-tion, by modesty. Modesty—what a beautiful word!"

But however valuable the Masters-Johnson documents are for the improvement of the national sex life, they don't incarnate the beautiful vision. The problem isn't that the projectors should have acknowledged that, as the literary men charged, the Sub-jects were "making fools of themselves," or were without taste or

---

child care, a return to the rigid, enforced suppression will be inevitable and mandatory. Otherwise the biological family will disappear and what other patterns of infant care and adult relationships could adequately substitute cannot now be imagined."

Speculation in this vein might have been inappropriate in the Masters-Johnson report. But that report was needlessly inhibited about underscoring findings with direct bearing on central domestic institutions. For a further discussion of Dr. Shurfey's interpretation of these findings, see the *Journal of the American Psychoanalytic Association* for July 1968.

, reticence, or were having their sexual needs catered for too lavishly. The problem is that, when at length the researchers undertook to deal with the *innerness* of their subjects, they offered up a false account of feelings, one whose omissions were as substantial as any found in the "cultural fiction" against which they inveighed.

Consider the passages about "Subject D" quoted above. The authors are speaking here, by their own claim, not about physiological reactions but about what it was like, in human terms, to be a Subject in this study. Yet their words leave the impression that the entire sequence of feeling can be expressed as a straight line progression from doggedness to surprise to gratitude. Understandable, perhaps, not to allude directly to courage, desperation, presumed humiliations, frowns of impatience and self-disgust (as when "coition [was] attempted without ejaculatory success"). Forgivable, owing to the need for sustaining a neutral tone, for the authors to translate the comments of Subject D and his wife into bureaucratese. (Subject D's wife probably didn't *state* that "subsequent to program participation my husband has been infinitely more effective both in stimulating and in satisfying my sexual tensions." And Subject D himself probably did not *say* that "I, in turn, find her wholly responsive without reservation.")

But unforgivable, and utterly unscientific, to pass out adman or testimonial simplicities as a substitute for an account of the whole psychological process of improving a sexual relationship—the subtleties and intricacies of self-perception in such a venture, the details of inward change, shadings, and redefinitions of trust and confidence, and subsequent characterological transformation. "Together they maintain that they have gotten a great deal more out of cooperation with the program than they have contributed, and they wish to continue on a long-term basis"—as a summary of the emotional and intellectual realities known by human beings in course of such a project, is this statement not as deceitful as the claim that "there is no such thing as sex?" Was it not unprofessional—not to say "fictional" or "mythical"—to set forth patches of backpatting uplift as a substitute for the full story?

How is the ordinary reader—hundreds of thousands of copies of Masters and Johnson have been bought by ordinary readers—to know, given these deeply censored case studies, together with the five years of silence that have followed them, that a full story has been withheld?

Again a cautionary word is necessary. Asking such questions doesn't mean lining up with the literary antisexologist, the critic whose hostility to the scientists' practice of expunging psychological contingencies from the records leads him to vilify sex research as sin. Neither does it mean ignoring the probability that the sex researchers included their uplift case studies in the hope of justifying their project and quieting criticism. It does mean asserting that the sex researchers' determination to praise themselves as courageous debunkers was obnoxious, and that the alternative to myth that they have thus far presented isn't much more adequate to truth than the myth itself. They do have an achievement to their credit. The sex lab proved that, in physiological terms, no significant relation exists between the size of the penis and coital satisfaction, nor any necessary connection between masturbatory orgasm and "frustration." The special physiological language it developed can be helpful to men, and does provide relief from the voguish porno puerilities of an "age of sexual liberation." Say it straight out: The laboratory situation creates a possibility of teaching people *what to do*. If participation by the scientific and literary intellects in each other's accountings of "facts" were the rule, as it ought to be not only here but in a dozen other critical areas of contemporary intellectual inquiry, the "achievement" would rouse more positive feelings than depression.

But as matters stand that feeling is appropriate. Founded as yet another venture on behalf of inclusiveness, the sex lab and attendant controversies testify that, for poet and methodologist alike, the whole human story is too much to face up to, too complex, contradictory, dense in variables to be touched in professional words. We are led out from a valley of deprivation into a valley of abstraction. We understand that the latter could be furnished, could be made comfortable for humanness. Sensitive men from both letters and science—call them scientific humanists—could do the job, provided they were committed to direct, patient, collaborative survey of problems, provided they were prepared to determine in continuous partnership when and where the methods of detachment can be productive, and when and where sympathy with contrarieties and delicacies of moment-to-moment personal response must not be foregone. But where are these men? They haven't come forth as of this moment, and until they appear abstraction rules unchallenged. We are offered no choice save to avert our eyes from full inward intricacy, comedy, dignity—full human nakedness—that which the great thinkers of the relevant past imagined men would someday learn to relish, not just endure. And our deep need—stupid ever to make light of it—for a sense of an ideal possibility, a ground from which sane minds can feel forward, tentatively, in the direction of a more habitable future, continues to go unmet.

Exactly What One Means

Expecting your arrival tomorrow, I find myself thinking *I love You:*
then comes the thought—*I should like to write a poem which
would express exactly what I mean when I think these words.*
—W. H. Auden

Why so, friend? mutters a voice like mine. With deepest respect,
why this Thing about exactitude? Don't misunderstand me, as
they say in Russian novels. I'm not intolerant. Poetry's good stuff;
terrible what they did to Cinna, don't shoot the nightingale,
doing the best he can, etc. But seriously: this endless yammer
about accuracy can become waffle, can't it? And abusing the
millions who settle for "I love you" and get on with the job is a
shade priggish, right? And it does on occasion happen, doesn't it,
that songbirds preoccupied with the one right word lose touch
with the Not-Me, with the world at large, a place never more
exciting than now, never richer for seeing, learning, wondering?

Oh, and one last point before being hanged for frankness: it
isn't only Philistia that finds the stuff produced by some of the
birds in question quite hard to read, *n'est-ce pas?* Might not the
sacred rage to express "exactly-what-I-mean" be at least part of
the problem?

As every schoolboy knows, the approved current answer to
such badgering neither trims nor hems. It declares roundly that
precision of meaning stands among the brightest causes of civili-

zation, and that the true heroes of any age are those bent most
intensely and faithfully in service of the cause. And there's
obviously something to the claim. A sense of heroic struggle often
is communicated by poets in the act of refining a statement,
qualifying, doubling back, complicating pat formulations, teasing
out terms that connect fully and freshly with dailiness.

And the resulting experience is by no means invariably grim.
Consider, for instance—one instance among a thousand—Kings-
ley Amis' "A Bookshop Idyll," a poem whose steps toward
"accuracy" lead also toward a charming human view. A browsing
poet stands in a shop thumbing the pages of an anthology of
verse. The poems by men, he notices, are stony, all about foreign
landscapes, Rilke and Buddha, the double vortex. Whereas the
lady poets in the book tend to drown in love. Dwelling on the
contrast, the browser first produced a smug notion about masculine imperviousness ("We men have got love well weighed up;
our stuff/Can get by without it") and feminine unprotectedness
(". . . the awful way their poems lay them open/Just doesn't
strike them"). He advances from smugness to cozy sentiment:

> Women are really much nicer than men.
> No wonder we like them.

Neat, cute, huggable—but rather more thought up than felt.
Impatient, he presses on another inch—and now a pretty payoff
comes. The part about women being nicer than men was, the
poet avers, evasive. I said it only to bury what those poems by
lady poets brought embarrassingly to mind—memories of my
own softness, my own vulnerability, time and time again, when:

> We sat up half the night
> Chockful of love, crammed with
>   bright thoughts, names, rhymes.
> And couldn't write.

Nothing momentous here, maybe, but nothing tiresome or useless
either: a commonplace ("Man's love is of man's life a thing
apart") complicated by remembrance; wit melting toward truth.

Or for another instance, consider the famous unwritten poem in prose that provides the epigraph—Mr. Auden's "Dichtung und Wahrheit," fifty paragraphs on *I love You,* fifty tries at clarifying relations between words and feelings, lyric and life. In theory a wearing project, in practice nothing of the sort. For this is a poet's pursuit of exactitude, not a pedant's. Tensions of mind and will are seen into with cool gravity during its course: "I should like to believe that it is some evidence of love when I can truthfully say: *Desire, even in its wildest tantrums, can neither persuade me it is love nor stop me wishing it were.*" But the seer doesn't hesitate to tell jokes on himself as he goes: "*I will love You whatever happens, even though You put on twenty pounds or become afflicted with a mustache:* dare I promise that?" And there is scarcely a single moment when this enterprise in precise definitions fails to entertain.

Even, indeed, when the costliest, most unjocular refining of meaning is in process, even when the reader is aware that a confrontation of one or another truism (Modern Man Is Rootless, The Age Is Corrupt, etc.) is becoming a painful self-encounter—even then pleasure isn't necessarily foregone. The central subject of rumination in James Merrill's "An Urban Convalescence" is Manhattan impermanence—streets torn up, buildings torn down, huge cranes "[fumbling] luxuriously in the filth of years." And an entirely serious contest is waged inside the feverish, inefficiently tranquilized East Sider who speaks in the poem—a contest between habitual lapses into cultural commentary on megalopolis and the impulse to speak an immediate and personal response to things seen.

Since habit is powerful (cultural commentary is the most honorable substitute nowadays for details of feeling), the contest isn't swiftly won. The stroller remarks that the new buildings do nothing for architecture. He remarks that the situation would be unchanged even if the new buildings did a lot for architecture, for they are no less impermanent than the old ones:

> The sickness of our time requires
> That these as well be blasted in their prime.

But always as he speaks in this too familiar tongue, categorizing, dismissing, the sense of an inner resistance is vivid, and at length the imprecision of such talk is directly confronted:

> There are certain phrases which to use in a poem
> Is like rubbing silver with quicksilver. Bright
> But facile, the glamour deadens overnight.
> For instance, how "the sickness of our time"
>
> Enhances, then debases, what I feel.

And this instant of clarity frees the man. Possessing himself newly, momentarily released from jargon, he perceives the immateriality of the quality or age of buildings, understands the difference between houses of brick and stone and true tenancies of life. The truth of his response to interiors weathering in public view can't be expressed in mutterings about cultural decline; battered houses, wallpapers flying, bring before him his own emptiness, not the culture's, show him the heart's deprivation, the heart's endless need:

> . . . to make some kind of house
> Out of the life lived, out of the love spent.

No jokes, no pleasant sallies, merely a steady movement away from cant toward the center of a genuine response. But the movement is highly affecting, and there isn't a hint of dry or airless inquiry in "An Urban Convalescence"—no surplus solemnity, no pretense.

Still, when all is said, it won't do to pretend that the chief point about poetic zeal for exactitude is simply that it isn't invariably boring, or that, in any event, accuracy pure and plain is a value. What matters much more is that people who insist on saying "exactly-what-they-mean" are insisting on their own human importance, claiming a uniqueness of being, asserting their pride. Implicit in Auden's comment that his poem must be written "in such a way that no reader could misread *I Love You* as I love you" is a belief in the supreme significance of individuality of feeling.

And Auden is scarcely alone in the faith. "Poetry is feeling," said e. e. cummings, "not knowing or believing or thinking." And this means that poetry is "expressing nobody-but-yourself in words," because "whenever you think or you believe or you know, you're a lot of other people: but the moment you feel, you're nobody but yourself." As for the value of expressing "nobody-but-yourself": well, said this poet, it's also "the most wonderful life on earth."

Perhaps. But it is just here that the negative voice wants another, possibly over-dour word. It wants, in particular, to remark the traces of self-indulgence and self-congratulation in the life in question. Is it not, after all, faintly fatuous, this swelling happily-approvingly in thoughts of being nobody-but-myself? What are the social consequences of faith in the almighty significance and perfect differentiation of separate egos? Is the sight of a man turned silent by depletion of ego so vastly more depressing then the sight of a man preening himself over his nonacculturated bits of being, the unsmoothed wart on his elbow, his odd turn of phrase?

True enough, the classic poetry of the immediate past—Yeats, Eliot, Whitman, Wordsworth, the others—is more than preening; in this body of work, self-certitude, pride, conviction of identity, separateness, personal meaning are struggled after, not assumed. And, true enough, poems still appear that are recognizable as human attempts to escape from the mass by knowing the full truth of massification—witness Denise Levertov's jagged, shocked, protesting verses on the superhighway:

> And the people—ourselves!
> the humans from inside the
> cars, apparent
> only at gasoline stops
> **unsure**

eyeing each other
drink coffee hastily at the
slot machines and hurry
back of the cars
   vanish
   into them forever, to
   keep moving—

Or witness those lines of Joel Oppenheimer's that, beginning with
gentle reflection on one woman, one pregnancy, one birth, run on
almost helplessly into the ugliness of *un*individuation, brooding
about:

   . . . all of us who turn heavily
on our beds at night. of the
   heart
which ponderously grasps its
way back, great sea creature
   caught
far up on the beach, a monstrous polyp or
jellyfish. of the lungs painfully
beating in used air to bring us
   back
sweating to face air. of the
   nameless
faceless images we dealt with,
   giving
our all. of the snorts and grunts
   and
great cracks of wind exhaled
   fighting
off the wild animals, keeping
   the beasts
at bay, while we slept. of all the
   legs
that might be slid between, all
   the
buttocks held firm and resilient,

all the nipples erected and
   tweaked
between thumb and first finger.
of all the bodies male and
female to be made love to
beneath the grinding of light,
air, darkness, all the
constituents and elements.

Yet the small reservations return and return. Conceivably their source is mere envy of the personality-monger, the self-advertiser, the triumphant eccentric, the mindless Giant of the day. But whatever the source, the result is, in one (overworked) word, a state of ambivalence. —Singers, in your precision is my beginning. Singers, you alone nourish belief in the significance of private feeling; you alone strengthen faith in the possibility of unique response. Right you are, the world of pure outerness, of unrelieved G.N.P., m.p.h., SAT, Rep.-Dem., prep-high, Brooks-Barney's is unbearable. Only here, only on pipe nights with the beautiful, thin books that nobody sends for Review or for Prepub Comment, that nobody wants Returned to Library or even Paid For (bookshops bill embarrassedly for poetry, doubting they ever stocked the thing that the slip says was bought)—only here does the inner self bloom, stretch, breathe, look about. There must be room for the inner self.

But how much room? How much human pride is supportable? What feelings in the noble "nobody-but-myself" can sanely be detached from the general cultural conditioning and called "uniquely mine"?—*I, I, I,* you keep saying, you voices in the thin, beautiful books. You *are* your precision, and I am the sense of personal difference created in me by my responsiveness to you, my love of your tune. But do you truly believe that this voluptuous dream of differentiation, this fine slaking of my lust for Uniqueness, does much for the survival of humanness? The sense of aversion, antipathy, remoteness from others that grows stronger in me as I read you, the distaste for public anguish and public joy and public words: suppose we grant that it built the present civilization, will it not also wear it down?

—Common stuff, characteristic contemporary quandaries, problems that can't be made to come out. They are, like everything on earth, merely more matter for poetry: reasons or occasions, maybe, for one or another precisionist to repeat to himself, in private, that, like Miss Marianne Moore, "he too dislikes it," and thereafter go on to explain—"exactly-what-he-means."

Reading, Writing,
Reality, Unreality ...

Success and fame at last: I'm invited to speak at the annual
meeting of "my" professional association—the Modern Language
Association, membership ca. 28,000—on the subject of English
Teaching, How to Improve. Do I know, without being told, what
is wanted for this talk? I do indeed. Something about Relevance,
assuredly. Something about Involving the Kids and Using the
Media. A sample turned-on test question perhaps? (Joseph
Andrews was the first Beatle. Discuss.)—My feeble mockery is of
course insincere: I'm pleased and flattered to have been invited. I
accept.

Still, there are some problems. To speak truthfully, I've been at
English teaching for years and years without ever having been
fully comfortable in the work as it's generally understood. Or,
rather, I've never felt close to the profession. Or, rather—why
trim?—I've felt downright remote from it. And not just from the
mainstream, but from the improvers and reformers as well, when
we've worked together at conferences. It's as though there were
two languages, one that's natural to me in the classroom, another
that comes forth when talking about teaching with fellow
teachers. Suppose, Famous Successful Doctor of Phil, suppose
this time you spoke from the center of your experience. Suppose
you laid out your inner assumptions—the ones that really determine how you work in a classroom. Suppose you said, Well, now,
just here and here is where we differ, just here is where I've had
hard going in the past with colleagues no matter what their

circumstances or mine, just here is where, despite my thousand assurances that I care about books, am no philistine, deeply believe in literary criticism as a significant act of mind, etc.–just here is where the tide of suspicion and hostility begins running too hard on the bow, and I slide off my point. Suppose, in short, on this occasion you were to take up spikiness, Stand Firm, say what you really believed? The earth would shake? They would censure the Program Committee?–And in any case (they can censure whom they will), in any case, what would it sound like? How would you begin? What exactly do you say when you speak the Whole Truth about yourself as an English teacher and lay about you, all boldness and megalomania, to abuse The Others? . . .

–Friends, you say, my first assumption is that it's by no means fatuous to attend to poems as real objects, autonomous, autotelic, free-standing. Everyone who reads decently knows the extraordinary experience of raptness, selfless joy, tranced involvement in the movement of a poem or story. Everyone who teaches decently knows that this experience–the entrance into the story as a world–in some sense "is" art, and that the moment we turn our backs on it and chatter about courtly love or the Elizabethan world view, there is no return to the spell, no fresh habitation of the work of art as "a world." And everyone also knows that there *are* ways of acknowledging the fact of a spell or an illusion. When we ask our questions about internal organization, point of view, rhetorical modes and the rest, we do show forth to our students our own fascination with the texture of the seizing hand on our wrist, our own interest and wonder at the ways in which we have at once been worked on and have ourselves worked in the encounter with the poem or story. And the uses of such acknowledgments aren't inconsiderable; students and teacher are elevated by them. They are momentarily privileged to care for something beyond themselves; they are seeking to actualize (I apologize for the cant word) the range of humanness which flows from the capacity of men to investigate their own delights and to arrive at the mode of consciousness that gives birth to standards.

The critical redskin who doubts the worth of such activity is, among other things, a man out of touch, someone unaware of the evidence about what repeatedly happens to human beings as a result of their effort to speak in acknowledgment of the spell or illusion of a work of literary art. Several times a year, each of us reads an essay about poem or book or *œuvre* proving in itself that a human being can be ennobled by such effort. Nor is it true that you invariably have to look hard for such work: Last year, for instance, two successive issues of one literary magazine provided just the sort of proof I have in mind. (I am thinking of the issues of the *Sewanee Review* that carried Mr. John Crowe Ransom on T. S. Eliot's "Gerontion," and Mr. Donald Pearce on Keats' Nightingale Ode.)

But to say this isn't to say that in most classes about structure and design (nature of the speaker, relations among images, linguistic continuities, interplay between dramatic units, etc.) that the aim of effecting a return to an experience, a reenactment, is sufficiently clear. Rather, these classes often resemble efforts to touch the bones of an object that never was alive, that never had laid a hand on anyone. The laws of anatomy are brought into the center of the classroom, and the humanness and livingness of lyric and narrative cease to count. And the English class becomes a place distinguished chiefly by total obliviousness to Whitman's great words:

> The process of reading is not a half-sleep, but, in highest sense, a gymnast's struggle . . . the reader is to do something for himself, must be on the alert, must himself or herself construct indeed the poem, argument, history, metaphysical essay—the text furnishing the hints, the clue, the start or framework. Not the book needs so much to be the complete thing, but the reader of the book does.

That such obliviousness can become a rule seems to me symptomatic of the English teacher's forced retreat to the periphery of his subject; his frequent inability to escape a community- and profession-imposed obligation to triviality—an obligation to names, not things; apparatus, not inquiry; the window rather than the view. When I speak of a "retreat," I am simply saying that I believe the English teacher isn't usually and primarily engaged in the activity of encouraging students to find the bearing of this book and that poem and this "composition" on their own lives; he is not using the authority of art, the actualities of the imagination, as they can be used. I believe the English teacher is inhibited about giving himself to the labor of drawing men into an effort to reflect upon and understand their own experience (a labor that art—and student composition—make much easier). I believe that while he declares allegiance to tradiional slogans about his subject, while he goes on announcing the supreme relevance of literature to the development of character, imagination, responsiveness to life, goes on declaring that books truly do "connect," he, nevertheless, concentrates in his day-to-day teaching on other matters. He busies himself introducing students to arcane literary hierarchies—the mystique of Great Books, etc. (Take a book, any book, *this* book.) The high school teacher and the college teacher function here in much the same ways. They assign on opening day a reading list—*Silas Lapham* or *Marner* or James Joyce or *Hard Times* ("You must have the trad, you see") or whatever. Everyone takes in, by implication, that this is the Subject: the first fact about literature is that there is high art and low, and Teacher knows the high. (The low is what other people read.) And Teacher will tell you which is which even if you don't ask. The key illumination he offers is that the low—often the student's own or "natural" choice—is beneath mention, does not organize life, does not lay an order over against experience, cannot be usefully attended to with an eye toward discovering *its* relevance to human life.

He, the teacher, introduces students to arcane literary hierarchies, and, in addition, introduces them to "objective" structures, designs, and effects. And he introduces them to the history of literature, the history of language, the lives of the great writers, their "philosophical outlook," and the development of literary form. (Shakespeare liberated the sonnet from Petrarch, John Donne liberated the sonnet from Shakespeare, then came the heroic couplet as released from Milton, and soon the Romantic poets protested against the heroic couplet on behalf of the sloppier quatrain, and then we have Ezra Pound.) And the teacher sees himself always as the enemy of a slovenly enterprise known throughout the trade as "identifying." He is bound by professional convention to oppose student involvement with the text, "identification with the hero," and the like. The student may "identify," God forgive him, on his own time, but please to keep the muck of your life out of my classroom. Yet, simultaneously, the teacher is telling himself that *of course* he's concerned with the relation between literature and life. But there is a "field" to be "covered," isn't there? We do have a discipline, a design to be held in view? And "they" do have to be shown what good books and spelling really are, do they not?

For an inkling of the meaning of the situation I describe, I believe you have only to consider for a minute what the teaching life of men in other fields would be, were they placed in a relation to their subject comparable to that of many present-day English teachers. The professor of chemistry would be a professor of test tubes, the professor of fine arts would be a commentator on paint and brushes, the physicist would be an authority on bouncing balls. Heat, light, electricity, organic compounds, energy in the one case, images of man and God and nature in the other—these would vanish as matters of inquiry, if an emasculation comparable to the emasculation of English were accomplished elsewhere. In place of a subject, an area of life, a portion of nature, or existence, the disciplines would be empty— contentless, dimensionless, insubstantial.

How much can be said about English before it was emptied of content? (I am still setting forth assumptions, and it will be over in a moment.) What is its lost dimension, its lost substance? The substance of English is dramatic and presentational, a fullness, an embodiment, a wholeness, not an isolate or a swiftly nameable concentrate: not energy, not heat. But, as already indicated, a way toward a true sense of this subject does exist—one that leads through negatives. "English" is not centrally about the difference between good books and bad. It is not centrally about poetics, metrics, mysteries of versification, or the study of balance and antithesis in the Ciceronian sentence. It is not centrally about the history of literature, not centrally about changes in moral and philosophical systems as these can be deduced from abstracts of selected Great Works. Still more negatives: the English class-room is not primarily the place where students learn of the majesty of Shakespeare and alas for Beaumont and Fletcher. It is not primarily the place where students learn to talk about the structure of a poem or about the logic of the octave and sestet, or about the relation between the narrator and author and speaker and mock-speaker and reader and mock-reader of the poem. It is not primarily the place where students learn to mind their proper manners at the spelling table or to expand their vocabulary or to write Correct like nice folks. It is not a finishing school, not a laff riot with a "swinging prof," not an archaeological site.

It is the place—there is no other in most schools—the place wherein the chief matters of concern are particulars of human-ness—individual human feeling, human response, and human time, as these can be known through the written expression (at many literary levels) of men living and dead, and as they can be discovered by student writers seeking through words to name and compose and grasp their own experience. English in sum is about my distinctness and the distinctness of other human be-ings. Its function, like that of some books called "great," is to provide an arena in which the separate man, the single ego, can strive at once to know the world through art, to know what if anything he uniquely is, and what some brothers uniquely are. The instruments employed are the imagination, the intellect, and texts or events that rouse the former to life. And, to repeat, the goal is not to know dates and authors and how to spell recom-mend; it is to expand the areas of the human world—areas that would not exist but for art—with which individual man can feel solidarity and coextensiveness.

So much for rough assumptions and opinions about where we are. If they are obnoxious opinions, they aren't so because held by an art-baiter. Their root is the simple sense that the teaching of writing and reading can become an enclosed, sealed-off enterprise, locked into terms of discourse which, whether identified as those dominantly of historicism, aestheticism, professionalism, or technicism, are too unrelenting self-referring to be worth praise.

I come now to my examples, intending to show what I complain against is visible in public reality.

Late last summer at Hanover, New Hampshire, some forty or fifty English professors from England, America, and Canada sat together, under the auspices of the Carnegie Foundation, the National Council of English teachers, and MLA to attempt to arrive at some good and just assumptions about English teaching. After a week or so of attitudinizing and speechmaking, people came to realize that they were being self-indulgent. The way to establish what one felt about teaching was to do some teaching, expend energy each before the other. So a committee chose a poem; our group was divided into classes of six or seven, and we were asked to brood about the chosen poem and then to suggest an age level or grade for which the poem seemed particularly suitable. With this grade in mind, we were to speak to: "What objectives would you hope to move toward in your classroom handling of the poem, what methods and approaches would you use?"

The Hanover crowd was not undistinguished, by and large; some citizens were well known throughout the profession. But the episode in question was, in my view, a disaster. Talk about classroom objectives degenerated almost instantly into rancorous dispute about Taste. How good was the poem? "I hate it." "It's bad Hardy, ekshly." (I shall come in a moment to "the poem itself"; the paradigm is what matters here.) "Don't you think something a *little* better could have been found? I mean, can't he *tell* the difference?" etc. Next: a question about the relation between the poem and the genre, dramatic monologue: What other poems might be put into the equation? Next: Would the poem be read in class, when, by whom, how? So there were demonstration readings, and it was agreed by the group that two of our number read well. But the question of the uses of the poem, the question how to place it in the classroom, how to set up vital relations between the student and these lines: those matters seemed more or less without interest. Here was a bit of poetry which, like many another bit of poetry, would strike an inexperienced reader as "clipped out" from somewhere, torn from context, quite mystifying at first glance, a kind of uninvited guest, all unexpected. Yet, even the probable surprise of the poem to inexperienced students wasn't enough to shake the discussants out of the vacuum of taste and genre talk. Before I come back to the poem itself and make a commitment about proper classroom objectives, let me deal, in similar paradigmatic manner, with a classroom situation involving writing.

We are at the same conference. A successful high school English teacher from Cheyenne, Wyoming, presents a paper about grading compositions—in particular, about how to teach young people to revise. The teacher's exhibit is a paper written on the theme of "an important decision." The answer in the unrevised and revised theme that we are asked to consider draws on an uncommon experience from the world of sport. It is, at bottom, a world not only of sport but of cruelty—cruelty which the student, because of his closeness to a local culture, is unaware of. The instructor, calling for revision, directs his energies not to the task of awakening the student's consciousness to the cruelty of which he is oblivious; instead he deals with the problem as one of "technique," and calls for more colorful, precise "details"; as though the use of writing isn't to seek deeper comprehension of experience but to tart up "theme topics" with Timese.

But, of course, from this distance the rights and wrongs of both episodes aren't visible. Let me first quote the poem just mentioned, Hardy's "The Man He Killed":

> Had he and I but met
> By some old ancient inn,
> We should have sat us down to wet
> Right many a nipperkin!

> But ranged as infantry,
> And staring face to face,
> I shot at him as he at me,
> And killed him in his place.
>
> I shot him dead because—
> Because he was my foe,
> Just so: my foe of course he was;
> That's clear enough; although
>
> He thought he'd 'list, perhaps
> Offhand like—just as I—
> Was out of work—had sold his traps—
> No other reason why.
>
> Yes; quaint and curious war is!
> You shoot a fellow down
> You'd treat if met where any bar is,
> Or help to half-a-crown.

What should one *care* about when one is teaching this poem? I must change the question quickly in order to fit it to my classroom, for I think it is probably a mistake to begin flatly with any poem, to begin any class as though the prime aim were to "do justice to the poem." I would say that the teacher does well to remind himself that the poem is the third voice in the room, and that he himself is not merely the servant of the poem, but the defender, interpreter, even perhaps celebrator, of the life and world of feeling. Saying it again: Only in his classroom are details of immediate, living, individual thought and feeling and response legitimate areas of interest and speculation. Well and good if he wants to say to himself: How can I show the organization of this poem? But he should add other words in the line of self-exhortation. He should remind himself that most men don't know what they feel, hence sometimes feel nothing; and the literature teacher and the writing teacher are men whose gifts and sensitivities are means by which others can be awakened to contrarieties and puzzles of ordinary response. The map of human relations and feelings known to the young is all Sahara usually; few marks on it except what the culture (or the rebel-culture) scratches—love of parents or hatred, pride in nation, pride in self, ambition, dutifulness, loyalty, unfocused cynicism. Flat counters, simplicities, socializing abstractions. Again and again, the work of imaginative literature populates the desert spaces, fills the blank tracks with probabilities of feeling.

At an interesting, though not primary, level, "The Man He Killed" is a poem about meetings, about strangers encountering each other, establishing ways of acting toward each other, controlling the terms on which they will be known. But the poem is first of all a small rendering of a single man's experience of fathoming for himself the relation between bits of his own behavior and feelings, and the grand impassive concerns of the machine of is-ness beyond him—state, nation, army. Hardy is always brilliant at imagining and revealing the responses of relatively simple minds to enormous events or issues. John Wain once said that Hardy's eye looks straight enough into homely, normal, workaday reactions to permit his reader to see how little truth there is in the notion that homely, normal, workaday reactions truly exist. A teacher with ability to retain control of his class while moving freely from conversation to text and back to conversation might decently and honorably begin with a question about how we place ourselves in relation to the state or nation. Do you ever have a citizen-feeling? When? Can you say much about it? Describe it? The Lincoln Memorial at night? Leaving New York harbor, returning? Watching an Inauguration on TV? What is it like to be a loyal citizen, do you think? What are the elements of this experience? Have you ever been in a quandary about where you are in relation to an Official Policy, a Public Decision, the Country itself? "This is my country"—how much ownership do you feel in the "my"?

I would think a teacher beginning this way would want to turn away after five or ten minutes, proposing a poem as another voice in this conversation. There need not be endless agonizing about a perfect reading or about the goodness or badness of the poem. Neither item matters as much as our opportunity to move with young minds to consciousness of how people go about making a sense of themselves as related in significant ways to the public weal, public choices, issues, wars.

But we won't move at all, will we, if we fail to do justice to the third stanza, sounding it as it should be sounded? More questions here. Shall we read it as though the man were answering confidently? No? Why so? Why is he not confident? How does he answer? You might say, with a sort of faintly overacted concentration, frowning, bemused, overacted cudgeling of brains, "I am taking this problem very seriously, because I happen to be (within my limits—and do not think I'm without pride, I've got as much of that as the next man!) a serious, independent, thoughtful person." The questions here seem to point us not only at the man's way of working out a quandary but at the art of the poem as well. For a great part of the latter does, after all, lie in the strained turning of the lines to follow simple hesitation and pauses on to the release of a wry, hand-lifted shrug. The movement of the words does indeed register the movement of a mind, a simple man seeming to think it out, seeming to "work something out for himself."

But we must get to the central point. How does the man "solve" this problem? Does he solve it? Here is somebody trying to fathom a public mystery: Why do I shoot and kill another man, under the sponsorship of the state? What does this fathoming amount to? Well, it amounts to a gesture and a tag: Life is paradoxical, "quaint and curious." The man meets his need by acting in a certain way. By doing a kind of homely philosophical turn. By making a kind of profundum-sound. By lifting a shoulder in a manner that says, We're not so dumb, y'know. We at least know we don't know anything and when we say that, we at least know a lot more than your super-educated blokes—them what thinks they know bloody well everything.

How shall we "finish" our class? Perhaps not with homage to a poem. We may trail off asking whether, now that we are familiar with the way in which questions don't get answers, we ourselves will be less inclined to accept our own pseudo-answers, our own postures of reconciliation, etc. Are we not protected? Will we know enough to press on to "real" answers? Why? Why not? And then at the end, what will the teacher tell himself? All I did today "in English" was show forth a little of the manner in which human beings face their puzzles, bridge the gap between their slim certainties and the complicated rationale of events, bridge it by accepting their socially imposed obligation to behave as though everything does finally add up. I have asked some questions that might oblige somebody, at some future moment when he is saying: Well, we know life is a racket—or a paradox—or a joke—that might oblige such a man to stay a minute longer inside the mystery, instead of cutting it off with the word "paradox."

And, I say defensively, in these actions, I haven't much defaced the poem. The stillness in Hardy's stanzas, the part of the organization where for an instant the poem becomes quite good, is the moment at which the poem bodies forth in a speech rhythm a certain expressive curve of hesitation, followed by release toward "comprehension." The achievement of the poem is to give formed substance to a human effort to comprehend what is beyond comprehension. The triviality the mind offers in such efforts is carried in the silly-rote patness of the sounds—*foe, so, foe, though.* The small messy cluster of rhymes introduces words as words into the equation at just the instant when the man is discovering a word as a word—*foe* is "just a word," somebody's taught word. Just a foe, just so. Right. *Foe's* the right word. It is "right" because there is no way to move out of the suspension of thought in cliché, empty sound, or half-smiling gestures of reconciliation.

But we are not teaching the poem in order to celebrate a snippet of craft. No, no more than we are teaching it in deference to "life" or to "experience." Our deference is to the formed substance that the poem has made—the reality of one single man's particular way at a particular time with a particular companion of masking incomprehension as "understanding of a sort," the sense of what it is like to inhabit the skin of someone at the moment when he behaves as though he believes he "understands" what in truth is beyond his power of understanding. Our class hasn't precisely been "taught a poem." It has been in a conversation about understanding and blindness; and while the best voice in the conversation is the poem's voice, it is that only because *we* took it in, we showed ourselves what it created and how that creation comments on gestures of our own. And (one last point here), the teacher's art, if the conversation comes to anything, doesn't lie in his mastery of the poem alone. It lies in his or her approach to the great vision of the humanistic investigator found in Kierkegaard's *Concept of Dread:*

> . . . just as the psychological investigator must possess a greater suppleness than a tightrope walker, so that he can install himself within men's minds and imitate their dispositions: just as his taciturnity during periods of intimacy must be to some degree seductive and passionate, so that reserve can enjoy stealing forth, in this artificially achieved atmosphere of being quietly unnoticed, in order to feel relief, as it were in monologue: so he must have poetic originality within his soul, so as to be able to construct totality and orderliness from what is presented by the individuum [student or poet, I want to add] only in a condition of dismemberment and irregularity.

Less needs to be said about the other instance I cited: the writing episode. I want only to say that it doesn't seem to me that the good teacher of writing can see himself as a tutor in the craft of adding details, color, vividness, etc. His obligation is to move the student closer to the thing, to find the talk that will create a subject for the student, create a need for utterance, an eagerness to name a truth beyond the truth begun with. Here is the original paragraph which the Cheyenne teacher read to us. It is about bullriding:

> I had been riding bulls for 2 summers and wasn't doing too bad at it, when I was chased up a fence by a bull in Thermopolis. This didn't seem to affect me and I went right on riding; however, in Douglas this summer I rode a bull, and bucked off; and the bull

came at me, hit me, then tried to bury me. After that I swore I wouldn't ride bulls again. In the same rodeo my buddy was riding a bareback horse and he fell under it getting kicked several times. Then I swore I would never ride horses or bulls again.

And here is the revision, produced after the teacher asked for more details:

> The day was on the chilly side. The sky was overcast and the wind was strong. Most contestants wore jackets when not up. Bull riding was the first event, and I was second out on a good spinning bull named Corkscrew. He was a big blue-gray brahma with long horns protruding from his head like his big sagging ears.
>
> I nodded my head and the chute gate sprang open, and I then knew that this was going to be no picnic. He jumped high and began spinning to the left as if he was going to screw himself into the ground. I was just getting with the spinning bucks when he ducked out from under me, throwing me hard on my left shoulder. As I was rolling over from the force of the fall my eyes caught the huge animal throwing up dirt with his front feet, preparing to charge. I jumped to my feet and didn't waste any time getting to the fence, but my ton and a half friend was right on my tail. His head was lowered and snot was streaming out of his reddened nostril.

The snot in the nostril does not, I think, change the bull. It is one more bit of objective timese, one more "balding" or "blue-eyed" or whatever, one more pretense that the viewer does not affect the object viewed. The right question to ask the bullrider was, perhaps: What about the canvas strips wrenched up under the animal, crushing his scrotum? How can you think of them? Have you thought about why the animal bucks? Why does the animal not shriek? Why do we do this to them? Have you imagined this pain? Why do you yourself and I myself not care very greatly about it? Here is a dreadful, needless affliction of torment—a creature backing, rocking, tearing itself apart in air—and we are oblivious to the shrieking in these motions. Why so?

Questions of this sort seem to me to be analogous to the questions I wish to ask about the poem. They seek to remake a situation for the reader and the writer; they seek to shift the relation between the writer and the subject, edging him closer to the thing, pressing for the human response.

Someone tolerant of looseness but, nevertheless, troubled by all this asks: What makes you believe every teacher doesn't do exactly what you've just been talking about? I would instance, in answer, the papers I have read in the bound volumes of the last few Yale conferences of English teachers; I see no point in quoting passages, and I do not mean to set up against literary criticism, but these papers are presented as aids to teachers, and they seem to me by and large to speak to English teaching in different terms from those just set forth. And then, too, there are the episodes I cited, two among scores, from a recent and reputable international conference of teachers of English.

Someone else may ask: How could teachers with a subject as exhilarating in its contemplation as English let it slip from their hands? Especially when so many great voices, not mere doctors of philosophy like you, Professor D., have said loud and bold: Study the *thing*. (Do not talk to me of artistry: Van Gogh. Tell me about the mudbank over there. Or Turgenev: If you want to know my stories, then know my *things:* "All the images rose up before me as things:" Coleridge.) Why should things—objects, feelings, situations—not stand in better with English teachers than they do? Nothing short of a book suffices to tell that story. There are enormously complicated community pressures toward innocuousness and toward a bootless "mastery of mechanics" (the citizen with no ideas, no vision of himself worth punctuating, but with a clear grasp of "punctuation mechanics" is the desiderated product). And there are a number of intellectual influences that are scarcely less important. One of these is the advent of special traditions of professionalism among literary men and teachers—first, the cult of historical research, later, the cult of design and structure. Another is the powerful thrust (coming partly through the Symbolist aesthetic) toward dismissal of the referential nature of works of literary art: The poem became a set of relations within itself, a fascinating clockworks that told no time. For different reasons, the student composition had already become something analogous—a lesson in the mastery of a particular progression of paragraphs, rather than a raid on the unexpressed. Still another distraction was the noisy, pointless dispute between historicists and new critics—an argument in which both parties were in agreement on a fundamental principle: Students should not be encouraged to study poems and novels as discoveries or clarifications or embodiments of life itself. (The teacher who chose up sides in this dispute had the illusion of opting for something "concrete"; in fact, he merely took on another abstraction.) There is, in addition, the tendency of some literary men of positivistic cast to aspire to the condition of scientist; in other words, clear out the human junk. Above everything, perhaps, there is the widespread and ignorant conviction that only the mindless can speak with interest about details of feeling. But what person who has ever sought intensely and responsibly to know his own feelings in a particular situation could accept an account of that enterprise as intellectually unchallenging? The surest proof of the excruciating difficulty of achieving consciousness of one's own or another's responses is the rarity of effort toward that end. It is much easier to settle for public cant and private self-deception than to reach for the innerness of a man.

But the present need, as I said at the start, isn't for etiological surveys. Neither is it for long ponderings on the possibility that teaching which recovers a decent interest in the life embodied and represented in works of literary art (and in student composition) will lead to loss of taste, critical inexactitude, ignorance of our literary heritage, dumbness before the wonder of language. (The love of a melody cannot be lessened by attention to what the melody expresses, the pieces of life set in order and related one to the next within the tune.) Nor is it useful to agonize about the possibility that to deal with substantive matters in the English classroom means decreasing the distance between teacher and student and accepting, as a normal classroom event, face-to-face, abrasive encounters of assumptions, doubts, and longings.

For the truth is that the gains that could come from releasing the English teacher and student into the living world of their subject hugely outweigh any possible losses. These gains can even be fairly expressed in terms of significant national interests. It is the free man's awareness of himself as possessing a distinct life of feeling, a singularity of response, an individual tendency in time, that alone gives meaning and relish to the idea of freedom. And in the contemporary state there are massive forces ranged against every small encouragement and stimulation of that awareness, forces blandly denying the dream of individuality and the dream of self-knowledge. The English classroom is, ideally, the place where the latter dream is set under scrutiny, understood, valued, and interpreted. To reduce the classroom to a lesser place, to evade the substance of English in the name of stylistics, correctness, acquaintance with the classics, taste tests, colorful composition, is therefore to deny youth a good defense against the fate of mass men.

What is being said here can be mocked, I must admit now at the end, as amounting to a merely therapeutic conception of the study of literature and composition. But there is nothing on earth, after all, that cannot be defaced with a *merely*. The argument that the right course for English studies or humanities courses is one that prizes the poem and the play as windows opening on a livingness that would otherwise be unseen and dead to the human eye need not run into extravagance. There is no implicit claim that any man can be "saved" simply by such views and visions, simply by talking about his own relation to the state before meeting a poem embodying perplexities in that relation, simply by being pressed to consider the torment of the bull as well as the "need for lively detail." The argument holds only that the teacher and student who speak together of the things that books make palpable, who tell each other what they see and why they believe or disbelieve their eyes, can awaken in each other a stronger consciousness of humanness than that issuing either from an absorption in metrics or design or the hierarchy of taste. Is it not a fact that whatever serves the interest of that consciousness—the interest of a man's awareness of the immediacy of himself—also serves the highest interests of the highest art as well?

Turning On and Off
with Student Rebels

They turn you on, the student strike-and-bust stories—*Red Flag/
Black Flag* (1969), the Paris tale as told by reporters for a
London weekly, *Up Against the Ivy Wall* (1968), by Columbia
undergraduate reporters, the narrative chapters of the Cox Commission Report. If you're a prof and your school hasn't been hit
and you've got a grievance, you read them hand running, excited,
believing, all hot-pugnacious-involved . . . Up against the wall,
Prex! Suck eggs, Trustee!

—There are funny bits, to be sure. A drill leader (Mark Rudd
or Cohn-Bendit or gorgeous Sauvageot) calls a command on the
wrong foot and piles a column of rebels up on the ground; an
emergency faculty meeting chokes on amended amendments.
And there are horror passages as well. (Bad in New York and
elsewhere, the "campus" bust was obviously worst at the Sorbonne—more fury in *flics* than in pigs.) But even in the most
hideous reading moment, a sense of heightened life and promise
hangs on. And when it burns off, as it does in the end, leaving the
rebels strung out in the bare air of their fantasy, the sequel is
nevertheless not depression. For there are lessons in these stories,
as well as excitations, and, as it happens, brooding on them
doesn't bring a man down.

About one excitation they offer—vicarious revenge—a critical
word does need saying. Perfectly understandable why faculty
types relish such revenge. You and three other chaps and some
students hustled, say, for six months as an "environment commit-

tee," inventing a workable substitute for a rotten fraternity system—whereupon The Trustees, blithe, lordly, misinformed, killed your proposal over a drink. Or you were invited onto a minor Trustee subcommittee—pals at last—only the group never met thereafter, the Chairman merely sailing your thoughtful suggestions over the transom to the Board for friendly unexplained dismissal. . . . With these or other remembered frustrations or humiliations in the equation, teachers can be forgiven for taking pleasure in the sight of administrative snottiness (Columbia- or Sorbonne-style) getting its what-for—sweating in phone booths, being lashed by foul (student) tongues, pleading with faculty fixers, grasping too late that "something dangerous is happening." But blameworthy or not, such pleasures aren't improving. Arrogance is universal in academe, nobody's exempt—and insofar as the riot tales muffle that truth, insinuating that teachers and students somehow escape the great Establishment Sin, they're bad for the moral character.

On other fronts, though, to repeat, the books are impeccably moral—meaning they teach as well as excite. The chief lesson taught is about the uses of interruption to thinkers, and about the deadness of intellectuality as routine. Strike days at Columbia after the first bust saw much larking about—sunbathing in South Field, pot festivals, and the like. But *Up Against the Ivy Wall* shows that students and professors in impressive numbers were also talking straight and hard to each other in this period about how to restructure the school:

> Students had time to spend long hours engrossed in discussions with the professors they had met in front of buildings during their vigils, or with the other students who had been inside the buildings with them. Freed from the fetters of habit and routine, students were able to work on the Strike Committee's many projects. . . . Some attended the Strike Committee's "free university" liberation classes; more met with their teachers in dormitory lounges, apartments near campus and on South Field to talk about the strike as well as their course material.

More important, during the insurrections themselves students won extraordinary triumphs over their own lassitude, complicity in is-ness, conviction of powerlessness. Both in the "communes" of Morningside Heights (Hamilton, Fayerweather, Avery, Math Hall, Low) and in the Grand Amphi at the Sorbonne, youth itself took in, half astonished, that civilization does begin anew with every child, and that the terms of substantive human relations, obligations, aspirations, are ever open to change:

> For the thousands of young people taking part, it was a delirious and unforgettable experience, one of the most formative they might ever live through. If the May Revolution was anything at all, it was this roaring mass of spontaneous student committees and assemblies running its own affairs.   [*Red Flag/Black Flag*]

> Now, insulated from the norms and forms of American culture by several feet of office furniture and barricades, the students inside the "liberated" buildings were able to create social patterns of their own. The takeover of the buildings had begun as a political tactic designed to bring about the goal of social reconstruction. It quickly evolved into the realization, on a small scale, of that very goal. . . . Students could, within the strike context, *make the decisions that affected their lives.*   [*Up Against the Ivy Wall*]

There were puerilities, naturally—witness the candlelight marriage ceremony performed by a Reverend Starr for student rebels in Fayerweather. ("Do you, Richard, take Andrea for your girl?" "Yes." "Do you, Andrea," etc. "I now pronounce you children of the new age.") And everywhere there was vagueness—especially in the proposals for educational reform. *Red Flag/Black Flag* tantalizingly mentions a "marathon debate from mid-May far into June, drawing in students, teachers, and artists in all fields," held by a "Committee for the Preparation of a Reform of Artistic Teaching" in France. Complaints are registered against art-teaching that's overprofessionalized, remote from general education, "cut off from living art." *Voilà*. What are the counterproposals, new strategies, new teaching ideas? Not a word, not a single word.

And yet despite puerility and vagueness the sense of promise remains. A frozen world unblocked, the gates of faculty-student habitude swung wide, young and old speaking seriously to each other, perceiving freshly the shortness and preciousness of the life adventure, aiming anew to make something of it by acts of mind . . . Only a murderous stoniness could read of such hours unmoved.

Where then is the fantasy, the silliness at the core? According to Charles Frankel, a Columbia professor lately returned to campus from the culture wars of the State Department, the fantasy lies in the notion that if you're upset about Vietnam, racism, poverty, or the general quality of life, the bridge to blow is College. Only a dreamer or a fool would attack "those institutions in our society of which [these] ills are least characteristic," says Frankel in *Education and the Barricades* (1968).

According to the Cox Commission, on the other hand—these are the patient lawyers headed by Harvard's Archibald Cox whom Columbia retained to find out what really happened in spring 1968—the fantasy lay in the belief of reform-minded students that civility wasn't a cornerstone of academic enterprise at its best. (". . . the essential postulate" for young and old to remember, said the Commission, is "that the university is dedicated to the search for truth *by reason and civility*. . . . The survival—literally the survival—of the free university depends upon the entire community's active rejection of disruptive demonstrations.")

And according to still others, the fantasy was a matter of false optimism. For James Ridgeway, for instance—he is the author of *The Closed Corporation* (1968), an attack on the American university as a "center of industrial activity"—the rebels' error would be that of failing to understand that change is now quite out of the question. ("It is too late for the myth. The universities were bought by the Pentagon long ago.")

But for most readers the rebels' key delusion will probably not seem to be any of these. The center of the students' "thinking" appears to have been the notion that, after you've liberated a few buildings on a main campus, or paraded about town (Paris) with a union mob, your revolution is done and done. In *Obsolete Communism: The Left-Wing Alternative* (1969), Daniel Cohn-Bendit argues that the Sorbonne uprising of May 1968 proved that "revolution is possible even in a highly industrialized capitalist society." And certainly it's true that, in Paris, workers and students did march together, and several joint student-faculty-administration committees did come into being, and various reforms of admissions policy, curriculum, exam procedure, parietal rules did come under discussion. At Columbia, moreover, significant changes occurred. No gym. An end to footsie with the Institute for Defense Analyses. New committees at work. Fresh efforts at communication with the Harlem community.

Still the dream of Instant Transformation must remain a dream. The reform of a university, as of most institutions, requires excruciating effort, wearing struggle against dailiness, habit, the bondage of ready-to-wear ideas. "The longer I live," said Péguy, "the less I believe in the efficiency of an extraordinary sudden social revolution, improvised, marvelous, with or without guns and impersonal dictatorship, and the more I believe in the efficiency of modest, slow, molecular, definitive, social work." But how exhausting is that work! How long it takes! "A universal, one might say *untiring* laziness pervades the world." And, further problem, the delicious memories of the liberation interval fade fast for those engaged in this work. ("The spirit inside was beautiful," says the Hamilton Hall girl about the occupation, squinting to remember. "There was singing, talking, dancing to music from small phonographs, watching TV, participating . . .") Which of us who never heard that music can contemplate without whining the task of creating new, genuinely flexible-interesting-joyous learning situations? "Preventing people from sliding down their natural slopes—what is it but giant's work?"

And there are no giants, just us—and the work hasn't been done—and the rebels are, as Grayson Kirk, in his thin-lipped rage, insisted, "transitory birds"—and, dammit, like every gang of kids, they won't pick up their mess. And they're forever inventing newer, grander messes to make. And they really didn't try to imagine the future as particulars of feeling—seemed to want eternal hate as much as they wanted revolution.

—But bless them bless them bless them, they did interrupt. Bless them for that. Against the enormous weight of habit, their own included, they set a strong shoulder, and shoved. *They inserted themselves.* Not for long, not for nearly long enough, and always with too much larking to too many "small phonographs." But the light they saw out the tunnel, the little music they made, these frail new committees, surprising quivers of guilt—in the line of growing points, pray, what else exactly have we got?

The Man Who
Imagined Imaginations

The author hasn't changed my life, doesn't qualify as a Neglected
Figure, wouldn't be thrilled (might be amused) at the idea of
being rattled on about for a stretch in print. He bears an unexcit-
ing name—Charles Horton Cooley. He was long dead when I
began reading him. (Cooley's dates are 1864–1929.) In his most
attractive book—*Life and the Student* (1927)—he set down his
thoughts on "our time," human nature, the university and literature in odd little not quite epigrammatic, often contradictory
paragraphs, four or five to the page. (Far from fretting about the
contradictions, Cooley relished them.)

And the circumstances under which I took up the book were of
a kind that often makes for edginess and hypercriticism in a
reader. (I was on a self-improvement bender, learning Sociology
on my own, studying "seminal thinkers"; among Americans in the
field Cooley ranks as a seminal thinker.)

Still, I warmed to the thing—Cooley's *Life and the Student,*
that is—from the start, and it hasn't stopped growing on me yet.
Partly of course this means simply that I'm easy with the author,
or at least with his most visible side—the prof side, the kind
voice, the alert head. Cooley was an attitudinizer who went
around setting traps for himself, but the fatuities he catches
himself in remind me of mine. He claimed that he hated faculty
meetings because of the parliamentary fidgeting, the distraction
from significant mental labor, etc. Since that's my supper-table
line too, I felt it when suddenly he needled himself into admit-

ting the real reason faculty meetings depressed him was that "I do not shine on these occasions."

He was in addition (so he implies in the book) the sort of teacher who's prone to exalted views of his own motives and work, seeing only the noble character-builder in his disciplinarian self, never the sly cynic or cop. Since again I'm that way myself, his excursions—in a chapter called "Academic"—on the meaner teacherly seedinesses also have, for me, an edge.

And, as might go without saying, I share many of his opinions about the wider academic scene. He seems solid (to me) on the question, Can a teacher be made into an administrator? (Certainly, is his answer, as easily as a car can be made into a truck: "Stiffen the frame and lower the gear.") I admire him for complaining, four decades ago, that "no teacher or official becomes aware of the student as a human whole; he is known only by detached and artificial functions." I also admire him for saying publicly—harder to do so then than now—that, since faculty and students have "somewhat different interests," the student is often wrong when he is docile, and right "when he does not behave as the faculty would like to have him." There's usually, furthermore, a blade in his irony, as when he praises the contemporary (1927) zeal to suppress radical ferment ("though stupid, [this zeal] should probably be encouraged as a possible incentive to rebellion"). Yet neither his feeling for the worth and separateness of the undergraduate interest nor his enthusiasm for social transformation sucked him into stereotypes (like ours) of The Student as surefire savior or hero:

> College students are not the homogeneous crowd that some imagine. As in other societies, there is a dominant type or form that more or less imposes itself upon the whole, but underneath there are variants, many of them maladjusted and more or less psychopathic. In the eye of each, if you look for it, you may see an individual spirit, a self, often only partly at home with its fellows.*

---

* No mystery about how Cooley came by his academic knowledge. Born in Ann Arbor, educated in Ann Arbor, married to an Ann Arbor girl, he climbed the faculty ladder in that place—the University of Michigan—and

But easy as it is for my prof side to cotton on to Cooley, the reason his book grows on me doesn't really have much to do with academic soul-brethren ties. The truth is I use *Life and the Student* as what's called inspirational reading; the book incites to optimism, and I'm vulnerable to the special style of its prodding. For one thing, there's little sentimentality in these pages, and no high marks for innocent or brainless virtue:

> Too long we were taught that good will was the same as goodness. We now see that most evil is done by those who mean well. What we urgently want is knowledge—true perception of the working of each part on every part of the common life of men.

For another, Cooley's vocabulary of uplift, while old-fashioned, is work-oriented and practical, nothing mysterious or godly to turn a person off. (Recurring phrases are "constructive imagination," "mental energy," "mental stability," "persistent cumulative labor," and the like.)

And, best of all, Cooley is longer on showing than telling. He does, true enough, have some general propositions to sell. Chief of them is that people should learn to push their minds to comprehend "personal" ideas held by others:

> Society is an interweaving and interworking of mental selves. I imagine your mind, and especially what your mind thinks about my mind, and what your mind thinks about what my mind thinks about your mind. I dress my mind before yours and expect that you will dress yours before mine. Whoever cannot or will not perform these feats is not properly in the game.

Or again:

> . . . the imaginations which people have of one another are the solid facts of society. . . . I do not mean merely that society must be studied by the imagination . . . but that the object of study is primarily an imaginative idea or group of ideas in the mind; that is, we have to imagine imaginations.

But that belief doesn't emerge as an abstract formula; it appears instead as a mode of behavior, a set of actions. The mind

---

died there, at sixty-five, having spent but a year or two of his life away from a campus town.

inside *Life and the Student* constantly puts itself under pressure to know and feel from some other position besides that which is habitual—to know how another point of view is held, what vectors of decency, viciousness, obliviousness, fear, or whatever hold even the maddest eye on its bearing. Cooley ventures into crazy jut-jawed anti-Semitism and speaks from within this obtuseness. He broods on an actor's minute-to-minute experience on the stage, speculating on its inner quality and texture. At one moment he spends himself imagining the anxieties of the thoughtful and sensitive man:

> His self-consciousness is awakened and intimidated by strange people. It is fear in the dark. Every new person is a fresh glass in which he is impelled to see himself. Hardly a child comes into the house but he finds himself imagining how he appears to it and wishing to appear well.

At the next he's smiling into the minds of two ladies who bump into each other on the street, each gotten up in a new outfit, each imagining the other's inner idea of her own splendor. And, far more commonly, he's working into paired self-images of the rich and the poor, blacks, whites, immigrants, natives, placing the innerness of the privileged at its precise distance from that of the others—for, as he says, "one sees into life only as he has the fullness of spirit to enter into it." Cooley isn't, in short, a stand-off theorizer about "how to know," how to sympathize, etc. His paragraphs are mainly acts.

And, as I say, these acts serve—whenever I think to remember them—as counters to pessimism. Pessimism about good works, for example—attempts to make yourself useful where the help that's needed is of a kind it's feasible to give. I have a small, paid job at the moment that takes me occasionally into ghetto grade schools in Washington, D.C., to teach. Coworkers in the project —two able young writers named Sam Cornish and Lucille Clifton—are black. Kids and teachers are black. None of us is wasting his time, and usually I take for granted that my "services" have value. But there are bad days. A middle-aged Ivy

WASP can easily miss the boat, act condescending, hurt some-body unintentionally, misunderstand a remark, make a tactless joke, read a face wrong, etc. etc. —Cleaver has clout at such times, a lot of it—Cleaver, Jones, Baldwin. You want to forget them and hear somebody encouraging, somebody saying, You can do better, can imagine more clearly, aren't locked in. Hang in there, Teach. Cooley, a calm coach, is the right medicine. Keep-ing him in mind meets a need and shakes off self-pity.

And the man is no less helpful in the other area wherein, for me, pessimism is hard to take—the work desk, the typewriter. Not to mince words, editors have been known to knock my stuff as hard to read. Too much brambly qualification, too much roundabout-again, fella, don't twist and turn so. Relax. I don't cave in instantly when this happens. I explain to myself that I'm out to represent "views of my views," hope to slip inside and tell how ideas or feelings fit together, within, for somebody else. But any writer, when knocked, is in the market for support, and Cooley is extremely supportive. He speaks up for a "persistent endeavor to see all around one's ideas, to assimilate them with fact from every standpoint, so that nothing of their meaning may escape." No "life made easy" character, a complicator not a simplifier, he's a fine corner man for writers whose "Let's try a rewrite" mail looks like mine.

Fair to ask: Why settle for so little? Is Cooley the only opti-mist, the only bearable recommender of imagination, complica-tion, and the rest? Nowhere a more powerful voice? What about Péguy?

The most powerful living writer on Cooley's themes is, to my mind, Hannah Arendt; issues addressed in Life and the Student —and in Cooley's other works—appear in a clear and profound light in many books from her pen. No greater crier-up of hard, imaginative labor than this analyst of totalitarianism, no stronger advocate of effort that "does not tire of interminable dialogue and 'vicious circles,'" that alone "bridges abysses of remoteness until men can see and understand everything that is too far away from us as though it were our own affair." In a superb essay on "Understanding and Politics," Miss Arendt says straight out:

Without this kind of imagination, which actually is understanding, we would never be able to take our bearings in the world. It is the only inner compass we have. We are contemporaries only as far as our understanding reaches. If we want to be at home on this earth, even at the price of being at home in this century, we must try to take part in the interminable dialogue with its essence.

The note is well beyond Cooley's range—not much tragic grandeur in *Life and the Student*. But the lack is made up for by the supply of specific workaday notions in his pages about how to "try to take part in the interminable dialogue." Tricks, hints, dodges, ploys—much of what you learn does, to be sure, come down to that. Homely matter. Cooley says if I stand "at the classroom door and seek the eye of each student as they come in I [will] get a human sense of them that makes it easier to talk to them. A strange crowd facing you is oppressive." And I chuckle —what a gimmick!—and am sorry for my need for such guid- ance. Still, I'm glad to have it. Partly for the thing itself—this ploy and the hundred others in *Life and the Student*, partly for the glimpse of the frail counterpuncher who's nevertheless ready to mix it with oppression, disinclined to break the habit of hope.

And here's the essence of it, finally, the secret of the closeness I feel—the scale of the Cooleyan struggle. A gloom-fighter, a chin- up lad, Cooley is nevertheless human and unheroic, utterly unintimidating. No "towering mind," not even a faculty-meeting star, cheerful man, "just a prof"—yet he presses himself, thinks he can get out. Looking across the table he says, "Living on a little requires genuine freedom of mind—meaning you've got to imagine otherness from within and see yourself from without— and push and push and push. Tricky job. Still it's possible. You work piece by piece, elbows in, hands up. Stretch your head, don't waste time arguing and contradicting, look to learn, try to *find* the other fellow as he's known to himself. You'll be fasci- nated, wait and see. Life will seem absorbing, you may wind up thinking something can be done." I want to buy that, as it happens, so I wind up rereading this little book.

Existential:
Sixties' Cinderella Word

Pop question: Can *existential* make it big?

Prospects were poor until recently. A foreign entry, heavy, hard to pronounce, fast in the forties, faded in the fifties, the word looked a foot too long. Worse, it came from philosophy instead of from showbiz or sports. And as for the timing of its sixties' bid—crazy. Camp, charisma, nitty-gritty, dialogue, relevance, thrust—jargonville was jammed to the rails with winners: how could a "newcomer" break through? Despite the handicaps, though, *existential* is breaking through. Improving its place steadily, unfazed by cheapening, inflation, or technical correction, it's closing once again on high fashion. Given a boost from nonlinear media, its future could be immense.

As might be guessed, adaptability plays a key part in this success story. Useful in a variety of fields, *existential* has won strong support across a whole spectrum of nontechnical writing—magazines, newspapers, and books. (In the space of a week this season it was used in public prints to distinguish revolutionaries from gamblers, rioters from students, party candidates from write-ins, and the ovum from sperm.) But other elements besides adaptability figure in the tale—in particular, an Image Factor. Embarrassing to mention that, of course; it implies (falsely) that *existential* is just another contemporary blur-word, no core of meaning at its heart. (The standard pop core is as follows: Existential, adj.—*Not-knowing-what-will-happen-next.* Cf. Norman Mailer at the New York Theater for Ideas: "It was existential [the

Columbia strike], because these kids went out and did something that they had never done before, and they did not know how it was going to turn out." Or cf. Steve Cohn, in the Amherst College literary magazine: ". . . the trick is not to know what's going to happen next, that's existential, that's being."

But embarrassing or not, image-talk is necessary. You can't understand *existential* today without leaving the narrow denotative band and seeing the term in its largest dimensions, as an item closer to trade names than to ordinary parts of speech. Like Marlboro, Mustang, or Ma Griffe, the word sings, has mystery in its nimbus, casts a shadow, evokes the gut response. Charged atmospheres gather at its mention—the unexpected, the reckless, the unconstrained, the spontaneous, the indomitable, the solitary, the purified, the intense, the elemental. . . . The "meaning" of *existential* lies, in short, in the content of the Existential Image—beautifully controlled intimations of safe audacity swinging round the don't-know-what-happens-next core. And, as indicated, the goodwill roused by these intimations already ranks as a major popcultural capital reserve.

Writers who draw on the capital aren't hung up about how and where to spend it. Neither are they oblivious to its potential as a prestige-builder—a means of instant sanctification both of oneself and the cause one favors. For Nat Hentoff the cause one favors is the Concerned Parents movement, pro-community control of schools—therefore he describes the cause as that of "existential education" in his column in *The Village Voice*. For Charles Marowitz (another *Voice* column) the cause one favors is that of the Living Theater, the La Mama Company and Tom O'Horgan —therefore he cries up *Hair* as "existential thunder." For Mary Ellmann the cause one likes is female superiority; hence in her *Thinking About Women* (1968) she identifies sperm as humdrum and herdlike ("jostling masses, swarming out on signal like a crowd of commuters"), and finds the ovum to be adventurous-glamorous-existential ("the ovum travels singly . . . in [a] kind of existential loneliness . . . a daring and independence").

Connotations of daring and independence are by no means the

term's only plus values. *Portentousness*—a sense that something grave and grand, though incomprehensible, is nigh—also enfolds the word. One is aware of it, a misty penumbra, in a *Commentary* essay by Diana Trilling, wherein instead of the flatness of "special" or "peculiar," we savor the excitement of *existential:* "In the meanwhile one's friendly neighborhood suffered in its own existential fashion and went unnoticed. . . ." One feels it, too, in an article by Robert Somma in the *New York Free Press Critique,* wherein *existential* stands in deliciously for "usual" ("negation, despair, abulia [are] not the existential conditions of super spades or super stars"). And the Reverend William Jones, of Brooklyn's Bethany Baptist Church, achieves portentousness by dropping *existential* in to replace *real:*

> "[State Trustee] Johnson was just a puppet. He was not a free man. The existential question is: Is Firman free?"
>
> [*New York Post,* December 4, 1968]

There is, as should be acknowledged, a squarish pop usage, one that takes the term as synonymous with phrases like "existing, that which is," or "pertaining to real life." In *Cinema Now* (1968) the film maker Stan Brakhage reflects on the Beat Generation as a "form of life which is destructive of the self," and recalls that he used to say, when asked to comment on it, "We've got beyond the stage of existentialism, we've got to the stage of desistentialism."* And the word does have a few snipers, characters who concede its prestige grudgingly or ironically, if at all. The dustjacket of a first novel published this month—*Yes,* by Bibi Wein—is sniffish about the book's hero on the ground that he "accepts love incidentally," and "romanticizes the existential

* Surprisingly, something of the same flavor—*existential* as pertaining to that which is, concrete life—turns up in Mr. Nat Hentoff's recent remark, in *Evergreen Review,* about the congressional education of Allard Lowenstein:

> As for transforming the Democratic Party into the agent of our salvation, that too is not in the immediate future as Allard Lowenstein, for one, is going to find out existentially in encounters with his party leadership in the House.

freedom he thinks he wants." And a recent Sunday *Times* maga-
ziner about the 20th Century-Fox production of *Che!* quotes an
extra praising the star of the film for seeing Che Guevara as a
businesslike "casino gambler" rather than as a wildboy "existential" type.

On the whole, however, disrespect is rare. When Michel
Crozier, the sociologist, invokes "the existential anguish of the
hippies" as an opposing force to the business-government faith in
the "science of decision-making . . . the omnipotence of reason,"
he isn't knocking hippies. When Michael Rossman, the New Left
leader, writes in the *American Scholar* that the student activist
movement is beyond politics, and works in "unstructured tempo-
rary groups in which the dominant themes are existential involvement and effective (potent) freedom," he's not lamenting the
Democratic decline. When Margot Hentoff declares in *The Village Voice* that her voting-booth decision to write her own name
in on the presidential ballot was an "existential act," she isn't
confessing she's a silly woman. When David Cohen, of Country
Joe and the Fish, tells *The New Yorker*'s "Talk" reporter that he
had a breakdown—"the beginning of the existential dilemma—I
just fell apart"—as a student at Los Angeles State College, he
doesn't see himself as a cloddish, insensitive chap. And when
Miss Renata Adler writes, in *The Times*, that Steve McQueen has
"existential" features, she hardly means the man looks bad. The
plain case is, to repeat, that *existential* has come through, bears
no negative scars, has a uniformly positive valence: at the end of
the sixties it means good, like pop knows it should.

For the student of popular culture, the questions arising from
this evolution are these: How and why has the word arrived at
its present state? What were the chief stages of its progress? And
neither question is quickly answerable offhand. It seems likely
that when the American *existential* record is thoroughly investi-
gated, significant contributions to it will prove to have been made
in two books by one author—*Advertisements for Myself* (1959)
and *The Presidential Papers* (1963) by Norman Mailer. For
while *existential* did have an early run in the forties, it dropped

from pop sight thereafter—until Mr. Mailer set it on a comeback trail. *Advertisements* was the first publication in book form of the author's ruminations on the Hip and the Square—chat that freshened the association of *existential* and romantic. And *The Presidential Papers* was no less notable, partly because it laid down the first pop definition of the word ("an act . . . is existential precisely because its end is unknown"), and developed the themes of existential glamour adumbrated in *Advertisements,* and partly because it was dense with suggestive new coinages— "existential legislation," "existential orgasm," "existential politics," "existential vibrations," "existential fatigue," "existential heroine" (Jacqueline Kennedy), to cite just a few. —But these notes on the *existential* past are at best scratchy impressions: the subject demands at the minimum a solid AmStuds doctoral thesis or two.

Nor are AmStuds' doctors the only likely researchers. For students of the history of philosophy this evolution also presents interesting problems, namely, How could a term be so efficiently, swiftly, ruthlessly stripped of intellectual content? What distinctively American gifts figured in the transformation? —Irrepressible American humor clearly had something to do with the redefinition. (Jean-Paul Sartre himself acknowledged this, indirectly, upon learning in 1947 that the American producers of *No Exit* had brightened the piece, and were playing it strictly for laughs. M. Sartre's churlish comment at the time was that "Les Américains ne comprendront jamais rien à l'existentialisme.")

And American production genius was also involved. Changing the meaning of *existential* sharply reduced the amount of time needed to produce a philosopher, even a "first philosopher of hip," and eliminated the need for mental labor. In former days talking philosophy of any kind required extensive training— profitless, time-consuming—in the analysis of concepts, and some consciousness of intellectual tradition as well. Talking existential philosophy was especially burdensome, furthermore, because on its strong side (the phenomenological side, developing from Husserl through Merleau-Ponty) this school conceived the philosophical task to be that of laboriously, responsibly uncreating previous philosophies, descriptions, perceptions, standardized structurings of experience, in order to begin the infinitely difficult task of knowing a thing.* For the American market a substitute was vital—some means of enabling people to sound philosophical without suffering the pain of thought. And the drive to meet this need helped to create the automated, or Hentoff, philosophical style—that device by which a man can think existential by signing his name, pulling the lever, uttering the word.

And finally, some degree of influence on the redefinition may have been exerted by American theories of experience and self-realization, and by the national idealization of isolated, autonomous, closed-system selves. European existentialists tend to be, if a frank word may be spoken, a shade chicken in their concept of freedom, stressing that, while I can realize my being in conflict with others, I must understand that others are themselves engaged in realizing their being in conflict with me; the resulting tension *between* freedoms defines the general human struggle and is the root of our need for balance. Americans are less inhibited, as the theme of creative violence in Norman Mailer attests.† We know better than to be distracted by complications stemming from too much brooding on the truth that, although human beings can be treated as objects, none is less than a

* ". . . we bypass [the world of perception] in critical thought—almost to the point of forgetting the contributions of perception to our idea of truth. For critical thought encounters only bare propositions which it discusses, accepts or rejects. Critical thought has broken with the naïve evidence of things, and when it affirms, it is because it no longer finds any means of denial. However necessary this activity of verification may be, specifying criteria and demanding from our experience its credentials of validity, it is not unaware of our contact with the perceived world which is simply there before us, beneath the level of the verified true or false."—Merleau-Ponty, *The Primacy of Perception.*

† Writing from a European, hence narrowly critical, point of view in a coterie journal called *Minnesota Review,* Samuel Hux recently remarked that "Mailer tends to force 'conflict with' to an insane logic, to change it to 'destruction of.' No longer does he realize himself in the *tension* of inevitable conflict, but in the apocalypse of chosen violence . . . This is not existentialism, but popular surrealism."

subject to himself. We also know better than to be gulled into the idea that thinking is a kind of experience; we know, as did our lesser forefathers from the beginning, that reflection is at bottom an evasion of or even escape from experience—and Experience is All. And this knowledge has in turn nourished the determined American effort to simplify existentialist key-terms.

As goes without saying, though, these matters of genesis, influence, etc. are at bottom purely academic. What counts isn't the nature of the forces that are shooting this word into the center of popular consciousness, but rather the simple fact that the word will arrive there, will have a life in pop usage. There are, admittedly, many unknowns in the equation. (How will the word make itself at home in social discourse? My unusual weekday-night third martini, for instance, formerly known as an extra drink—will I come to call it my existential belt?)

And there will also be, in time, some sadness. Older types, witnessing the slow descent of the term into phone-book listings—Existential Bagel, Existential Body and Fender, Existential Casket—will keen to each other, asking how a word could have been so corrupted. How could such rot be taught? Learning without studying . . . Thinking without thought . . . Philosophizing without wisdom . . . But this elitist rant, this maundering about yesteryear, won't for an instant turn the trend. For way out on the what-comes-next precipice, free, giddy, gutsy, orgasmic, alone, there's no nostalgia, Pops, no looking back over the shoulder—so man like uh y'know what cat in that crib *could* give a good existential goddam?

In and Out of Universal City

Bad moment for bringing out a new novel. Especially bad for a little book, familiar pattern—love, renunciation . . . Current Critical Trend Unfavorable. New Involved Journalism is all the rage. Involved Journalism is a personification of a vision, says Nat Hentoff (following Norman Mailer) in the *Evergreen Review*. "Who needs fiction?" says Professor Kazin in the *Atlantic Monthly*. "Who needs fiction in order to learn what is constantly reported by . . . the magazines, newspapers, college textbooks, and television set?"

—The line is hard to dispute. You want to say: "Involvement is a cage. Freedom is precious. Stories liberate." But merely saying so—it sounds whiny. What's the point? And as for demonstrating, actually trying to show where and how storymaking (and reading) can straighten people out, keep a man in one piece: could you even begin to do that without soaring into hubris—or tailing off into another tale?

The time is early May, close to the end of term. A foundation aide up from New York talks awhile in my office and then offers a gig. Fly out to Hollywood, observe some TV film-making, write answers to a few questions about the production dynamic, supplies of unused talent and imagination, etc., and add any thoughts bearing on the immediate business (the immediate business is Educational Television, Methods of Improving). The trip can be scheduled in reading period, guidance on "the coast" assured (an independent producer attached to Universal City

175

promises to cooperate). As for—oh, yes—money: we're staying in tight on this, but "a skinny hundred a day and expenses," will that do? . . .

The flight west (at the end of the month) is cozy, and I settle in on a Sunday night at a motel I've stayed at before—a block or two off Hollywood Boulevard, on the corner of Yucca and Something Else. (I'm not totally green. Behind me a year or two is a stretch as a writer-consultant in ETV, and a turn, before cameras, as an interviewer—in Hollywood, at that.) In the morning I go to work. I drive out to Universal City, meet my people, observe shooting on sound stages and the back lot, attend a script conference, a casting conference, a rap session and a gabfest, and begin "interviewing" producers, writers, coordinators, directors. Succeeding days are the same, and the notes pile up. ("Carol, darling, take your own time to sit down. Don't feel obligated to do it on the cue." . . . "Okay, it's *between* a rewrite and a polish." . . . "Are you going to eat that during the shot?" . . . "We need an inch under Ben." "Give Ben an inch and he'll take a mile." . . . "Roll 'em and go." . . .)

On toward dinnertime in the evening I walk over with the producer and his helpers to the projection room to watch the day's prints. (The footage is for *Run for Your Life*, a serial dramatic show about a young man with a year to live.) Afterward, sliding out of most invitations, I drive back to my motel, swim in the pool, mix a drink, eat alone, late, at this or that Pow Beefhouse along La Cienaga, and return home to work for an hour, pulling notes into paragraphs. Several days of this and I say my thankyous, pack up, and fly home. My "report" takes a weekend to finish (the foundation man likes it)—whereupon exams come in and the gig's up. . . . A trip, another carbon MS in a manila folder, a vanished check—day in the life of a culture reporter/professor . . . The story in theory ends here.

Suppose for a moment, though, that we wanted to go on with it—in the New Style, in Involvedese—with an eye to clarifying differences between new journalism and old novels. Could it be done? Is there a formula to follow? Guidelines for tyro In-

volveders? Hints? Rules? The answer is Yes of course, rules a-
plenty. In some particulars, indeed, the forms and conventions of
Involvedese are as tight as those of an aubade. (The conventions
include a set tone—conscientious embitterment; a set conflict—
Good Guy vs. Bad Guy within the reporter; a set pattern of
character development—the reporter is first a clown, then a heel,
then a seer, and a set climax or reversal or peripeteia—exposure
of the Involved Audience's vanity and hypocrisy.) —But why so
many words, as the wave said to the fisherman. Let's run the
junket through the involving machine and look at the scenario
that comes forth.

The first sight, naturally, is my public Universal City self,
angled to reveal a naïf, a Country Joe clownishly enjoying the
local magic, sloping about in a mist of stock responses. . . .

Item: a projection-room audition. After the dailies, the producer watches clips of starlets—casting is incomplete for a seg-
ment due to start filming in the morning. A face pleases him.
Backwind: he looks again. The girl speaks only a single line in
the clip. Striking wide eyes. "Get her," is the word to the casting
people. They set out on a telephone search. My heart races. I'm
hot for the sweepstakes: will A Star be born? They give up after
half an hour, and in a different but still charged mood, I think:
Sad, sad . . . Poor child. So near yet so far. Who'll ever know?

Item: A moment on the sound stage. Star and ingenue playing
to each other. (PAUL [almost a whisper]: "I'm sorry, Kate. I'm
sorry." KATE: "Oh, Paul . . . I've never blamed you—") Beautiful. I love it. I sigh with the ingenue, turn away with her, share
the inexplicability of things that keeps them from life together, a
future. . . . The director snaps his fingers, signaling the end of
the take, and delightedly I catch a glance—shy? approving?—
that passes between Star and girl. They like each other, then?
They're together, really together? I'm in rapture.

Item: Script conference. A new young director calls on the
producer to complain about the logic of the script he's to direct
the following week. A recent Harvard grad, producer of the

undergraduate version of Kopit's first play. Attractive, personable . . . I don't follow the talk closely enough—miss my chance to find out how sharp the lad is, whether he's another slumming Harvardian or someone earnestly trying to redeem his assignment. Plain enough why I wander off: "in my heart" I already know the score. He's a Harvard, isn't he? That means he's okay. Harvard in Hollywood sticks up for integrity, and rightly so. People respect people who stand up for themselves. You're damn straight. Up quality! Up taste! Reinhart!

—Well and good: we've got a tease and a theme—reporter as nit. It needs underlining and development. More confession, more personification of the vision. How about a backward glance, like so—

I've always been a boob out in Hollywood. I gorged on stereotypes the last time too. In my educational telly days, I plumped for a D. W. Griffith bio-special that presented the man as a noble artist-voyager afloat on a sea of muck. (Camera tight on bronze Hollywood Boulevard sidewalk star bearing Griffith's name, as the voiceover laments—during pullback to twoshot—the chewing gum that pedestrians grind into his memory.) Nor is that the half of it. I'm forever sucking up to local values out there. It's true. Was I not ecstatic—on this trip—when asked for my views at a script conference? Did I not become embarrassed about my drab professorial rented compact car? At home it's easy to be properly sniffish about posh car conspicuousness, but out there— The truth is, I'm *extremely vulnerable to corruption.* Going in and out of the gate I avoided the guard's eyes; I was downright furtive.

And the night I accepted an invitation to dine with a Biggie—more sin. We climb out of the chauffeured car in Bel Air; I follow the cigar through the voluptuous house, single-file line of march, children, maids, dogs, hanging on, hoping to delay our passage. (Same bit every night, the man says, patting this one, shaking that one off.) And we slip out a side Dutch door through a lush garden to a pool house—domesticity left behind, sweet young bird waiting on pool terrace to make drinks. "We" three eat by ourselves, chuckling, happy, *yé-yé,* we here, they there. . . . Did

I speak up for the family? for good solid middle-class values? I did not. I read my way deep into this alien pattern: two worlds, eh? servants and children in one, yes, grown-ups separate, hmmmm. Mmmmmmmmm?

—Pause here, frowning—a moment of perplexed search for self-understanding. Or for self-justification or for a rationalization. Perhaps my finkery was actually good manners. (Would it not have been rude to confront hospitality with a solemn endorsement of family togetherness?) Perhaps the sucking up was determined in my youth—spells cast over me in the Fantasy Theater off Sunrise Highway in hometownville. Saturday afternoon, enfolded, glass bell over me, hurrying away from the flicks. Safe in the schoolyard, screened from sight, I fight the air and smash chins (if the flick's been Gable or Garfield), or, if it's Sophisticated Comedy, I light my Sensation with Bill Powell's insouciance and speak out in Cary Grant's voice. Having once adored the glamour, having once given up my whole self to it, having once become a mere echo, could I have expected to break out of myself in the real Hollywood? . . .

—Okay: we've made it to the middle. Our line thus far—for the Involvedese Scenario—is that in the daytime Uni-City was Fun City for me. A place where my mind cut off altogether and I shuttled about from one act of identification to another—fool, fraud, boozer, comic, happy sunshine sycophant.

But at night—here's a key moment: we're turning toward The Deeper Guilt—at night and the following weekend I stopped shuttling. Another character rose up in me and held the floor: the foundation fink, the "culture critic." I try to be fair to him at first. I say, In a way the culture critic was doing the best he could. We have to have people like that. It's a condition of The Culture. The Culture Critic had specific questions to answer about morale, taste-levels, and the like. He was just doing his job. Ah but no, dammit. (This is an emotional outburst.) I *loved* the job. I was shameless. My behavior as Culture Critic was downright treacherous. Did I so much as hesitate, for instance, before invoking

alienation theory behind my hosts' backs? No, I did not, witness
this paragraph of my report:

> . . . no community interest or shared sense of responsibility for the
> finished segment of a series show unifies production staff and per-
> formers, directors, men on the set. . . . The executive producer. . .
> and his immediate associates are usually visible to others chiefly
> in entrepreneurial roles: they are artificially drawn off into a separa-
> tion—as "coordinators" of ungraspable multiplicities. . . . Stereo-
> types of art versus business harden. Tensions, frictions, suspicions
> deplete trust. Feelings of powerlessness burgeon. . . . The per-
> former retreats into a reductive sense of himself, experiences no
> sense of control over the production as a whole, and at length
> dwindles into self-pity. . . .

Furthermore I savaged the product itself, never hinting how I
dug The Stars:

> Run for Your Life is fairly described as a fantasy. The shtick is the
> imminent death of the hero, which places him beyond ordinary
> moral chastisement (whatever the behavior, decency would feel com-
> pelled to forgive it). The hero has a positive obligation to sin. He
> was created as a sophisticated, attractive, appetitive hero—and if
> such a figure were to form a permanent relation with a girl, he would
> be guilty of self-indulgence, or even of cruelty itself. The character
> of his situation therefore establishes or suggests a world in which
> promiscuity is probity—and that world is scarcely unwelcoming to
> mass fantasy and desire. If the imminence of death were constantly
> stressed, true enough, the fantasy would be contained or qualified.
> But here again the executive producer is alert—too alert—to the
> substance of the program's appeal. He remarks that he avoids scripts
> which make much of the death theme and turn the viewer's face too
> blankly toward reality.

Even at the moment of final survey, I held to my lying con-
descension, and spoke in pained distaste:

> There are elements of garish pseudo-sophistication in various seg-
> ments of Run for Your Life, and the dialogue abounds in three-dot
> waffle. (Sample provided.) But the precedents for this warmed-over

Sagan—if not for promiscuity and bloody socking matches—in the radio soaps of the thirties and in sentimental ladies' fiction of the late nineteenth century are past counting. Neither show nor hero is an inexplicable phenomenon, a freak of culture. Both are continuous with America, part of a seamless cultural whole. What is unappetizing about them is also unappetizing about Ford Galaxies, Holiday Inns, Hollywood Boulevard between Highland and Vine, the teary-sincere orator in LBJ, the smile of the airline stewardess, *Valley of the Dolls,* many commencement speeches, and perhaps half the articles in this month's issues of the "quality" magazines. Style, discipline, clarity of thought, fullness of understanding are lacking—and the heart is nevertheless somehow vaguely felt to be in the right place.

Am I not a wretched soul to have set myself up so high! Am I not a hypocrite to have left my own clowning goof-off response so far behind!

—Time for the kicker, the close. We need a moment wherein "I" the Involved Reporter get it in the ear, am *caught out* in my fundamental insincerity and guilt. No problem: life supplies the *shtick.* Within months of my trip to "the coast" my two opposing selves—Detached Critic and Secret Showbiz Buff—clanked against each other noisily in public, did they not? Knowing only the part of my nature that I cheesily dressed out for them, the producers of *Run for Your Life* trustingly wrote me into one of their scripts. Ben Gazzara, Star, takes down a book "By Benjamin DeMott" from the shelf of a new girl friend's apartment, and comments in a way suggesting that anyone who reads my work must be highly educated and a person of Natural Taste. At the time I was asked to release my name for this use, I was touched. Showbiz, ah, Showbiz! But time passes. They catch up with you. At the end of a class last spring, a spiky straight-A student wheels up to incorruptible me and says, You were on TV last night, a real lousy show, how come? Feeling the tide of his disillusionment (Say it isn't so, Prof), I hang there suspended, as I hang here in the final paragraph of this swell piece of Involved

Reportage. I hang suspended and then pretend puzzlement, not having the courage to face him.

But though I acknowledge no complicity, turn away, I am—at least for an instant—nailed. And you know it, Reader, don't you? You wanted it. You want to whip me. Chew me. You're rejoicing because I got what I deserved, right? So you see? *You're another.* No compassion. We're all [obscenity] together and it was ever thus. Whereupon we

GO TO BLACK

As should be said at once, an essay that fleshed out the model above with appropriate details, intensities, and dirty words wouldn't by any means be useless. It could put a reader in touch with several bits of conventional wisdom about contemporary life—as for example that even on holiday people see their inner world as conflict-ridden; and that a man's fantasies rouse contradictory responses—joy, shame—inside him; and that the objectifying culture which seeks to neutralize "the personal" imposes strains and falsehoods; and that, responding to this pressure, people discipline themselves, separate their parts and arrange them in hierarchies, in order to create a viable professional self.

But despite these reminders, these occasional gestures at something beyond the Involved Reporter, the actual function of such writing isn't, as the small scenario should show, to bring a world into general view. On the contrary, the function is to explore a literary mode of self-suspicion. The explorations are often witty, sometimes intense. There is a certain play within the tone of embitterment. It's flexible enough to accommodate ruefulness and embarrassment (see Andrew Kopkind on serving *Time* in the *New York Review of Books*), as well as earnest, caring, self-chiding (see Murray Kempton defining, in *The Spectator*, his feelings of guilt after the murder of Bobby Kennedy). A disciplined reporter occasionally makes his guilt felt in a piece without explicitly focusing on it—see Tom Wolfe's piece on a father-son, adman-hippie confrontation in the Village (*The*

Kandy-Kolored Tangerine-Flake Streamline Baby), or Rex Reed's account of a family Sunday at the Paul Newmans', unaccredited sightseers and tourists milling outside while Reed is well treated within (*New York Sunday Times*, September 1, 1968).

But too often the impression, no matter what the precise tonal register or level of discipline, is that form has preceded substance. Selection of details both from outward events and inward response lights up discontinuity, opportunism, insincerity; personal rumination curves repeatedly, deterministically, toward the occasion when the reporter "finds himself out." Conscious from the start of an obligation ever to inch his way toward a more solidly cynical idea of a person, the writer speaks always with a self-deprecatory tic.

The tic has a history, naturally, and a sociology as well. Reductive versions of humankind have been standard items in Western thought for longer than a century. Psychiatry has enlarged the market, as Seymour Krim—his essay "Making It" (1968) is a landmark in the development of Involvedese—once pointed out:

In the climate we all make it in, the age of suspicion, putdown, sneer, needle, it's almost inevitable that a swinging person is going to probe himself for the hidden motivations in the way he acts, makes his little scenes. Introspection is the private playground of every brain around, there's no escaping it, and especially in New York where psychiatry has gotten such an incredible play is there a used condom of doubt that drags down every full-hearted gesture into the subway mire of the psyche's triple-dealing [*sic*]. Face it, man—nothing is safe in our world from the meanest interpretation, nothing is pure or uncomplex, nothing but *nothing* escapes from the enlarged vocabulary of analysis that our quick and unhappy minds grind out for sheer dissonant sport.

And the appetite for cynical views of the person is now fed everywhere in the media. Think of the endless series of Feiffer cartoons (Instant John Osborne, Instant Underground Man) showing sad-faced middle-class types abusing their moral character, and then being congratulated by their audience:

Your Honor [says a Feiffer character in panel one] . . . Ladies and
Gentlemen of the jury [panel 2] . . . I have great potential but
no follow through [3]. . . . I have contempt for the values of
success but I secretly hunger to be successful [4]. . . . I don't
know what love is, which is why I avoid all serious relationships
[5]. . . . I make a great show of interest in other people but I'm
really only interested in myself [6]. . . . I've never deliberately
hurt anyone in my life but I always feel guilty [7]. . . . I throw
myself on the mercy of the court [8]. . . .

In the next-to-last panel the jury speaks:

The jury finds the defendant a fine, insightful person who is not
afraid to be brutally honest with himself.

And in the last panel the man departs, slick, buoyant, smug in
briefcase and cigarette holder. "Justice triumphs," is his conclusion. The message is: Self-love is a disease beyond remedy. You
cannot confess without strengthening your sense of invulnerabil-
ity. "He who despises himself esteems himself as a self-despiser."
The evil in me is beyond my capacity to name and know. From
the trap of guilt there's no possibility of escape.

Or think of the insistence with which the same ground theme
sounds in the work of the literary masters of Involvedese—witness the central passages of Norman Mailer's *Armies of the
Night,* wherein the writer details his guilt at not spending
another night in jail:

. . . a failure of nerve always presented the same kind of moral
nausea. Probably he [Mailer] was feeling now like people who had
gone to the Pentagon, but had chosen not to get arrested, just as
such people, at their moment of decision, must have felt as sickened
as all people who should have marched from Lincoln Memorial to the
Pentagon, but didn't. The same set of emotions could be anticipated
for all people who had been afraid to leave New York. One ejected
oneself from guilt by climbing the ladder—the first step back, no
matter where, offered nothing but immersion into nausea. No wonder
people hated to disturb their balance of guilt. To become less

guilty, then weaken long enough to return to guilt was worse than to remain cemented in your guilt.

"That passage," says Mr. Hentoff, not only "draws you in," it "brings you the news about the rest of your life." And again the news is that "for the rest of our life" we must wear another man's dirty shirts.

News of this kind resembles dogma more than things as they are, and some who are in close touch with their own full human complication are likely to resist it. Sustaining an uncomplacent, non-beamish resistance is impossible, however, without protection from cynicism about the person—and what protection can be found? I can mumble commonplaces and truisms at guilt-mongers. I can talk to myself about the connectedness of human parts, about the interdependency of self-love and self-criticism, about the intimate relation between human fantasy and social hope. I can remind myself that the common (and absurd) day-dream of escape from conditioned existence into Absolute Integrity or Beauty or Guiltlessness is at the same time a force charging me to invent new models of life, and reinvigorating old standards of assessment. I can lay it down that men's dignifying severities of self-scrutiny have roots in indulgence, that responsibilities begin in irresponsibility, and that the compulsion to believe the worst of ourselves—the style of conscientious embitterment, dutiful self-hatred—is in fact a vanity, a fleece-lined hair shirt, bearing no relation to genuine humility or genuine pride, and invariably deflecting both understanding and the will to modify or re-create the conditions.

But, expressed thus, these truths are the merest chat, worthless until the meaning is known from inside. And the case is—coming at last to the point—that there are few surer ways into that meaning than through imaginative writing. To say this, to say that fiction alone draws us out from the cage of self into caring, knowledgeable concern for the life that is not our own, isn't to claim that novelists and storytellers are untouched by high-fashion self-hatred. Neither is it to say that journalism by literary

men never draws a person out in the fashion described. (There
are hints of conscience-nagging in George Plimpton's *Paper Lion;*
the writer once or twice damns himself for an interloper, etc. But
because his subject permits lightheartedness, and because he
himself has virtually a lover's feeling for the charm of his own
fantasy, he can bear to let his reader see beyond him.)

It is to say, though, that creating a story, whether as writer or
reader, is an act capable of liberating people from the boring
predictabilities of self-regard. That creation is a means of living
into the interdependency of "best self" and "worst self," and of
pushing beyond artificial borders, beyond official moral simplifi-
cations of human motivation, beyond this year's lit-establishment
tone and style of self-assessment, into a clearer, denser, fresher
world. Reading or writing, I indulge my desire or need to be
someone else, to be a different person in a better world—and am
reminded that this desire is at once an indulgence and a moral
distinction—and am lifted (briefly, that is true, only briefly) by
this "literary" experience to a kind of behavior both as judge and
as fantasist that possesses unfaked dignity. I oscillate between
permissible identifications with other human beings and an at-
tainable detachment. I sense contrarieties pressing inside the next
man. I'm elevated by the act of judging deeds that aren't mine,
but that are yet known to me from within.

And it *is* the judgment—that act of judging—that's most exhilarating. Reading and writing fiction is far from a murky love-in
or flower kiddies' ball. It is an act requiring sympathy, since
"understanding" is the goal—but not an extravagant sympathy of
the kind that chokes the sense of justice. Reading *Anna Karenina*
I'm not simply bewildered or amused that Oblonsky can at the
same time be wretched about his faithlessness to Dolly and
tickled by some wisp of recollection of the "bewitching" gov-
erness. I don't simply take this response or conduct in a forgiving
spirit, or regard it as a determined event, inescapable. I come at
its inevitability from within. I feel the regrettable yet, for him,
oddly pleasing limitlessness of what we cannot control. I understand that the conscience that pains Oblonsky also delights him

by reminding him of his personal attractiveness. I am unremittingly aware of the reciprocities of what is called "virtue" and what is called "vice," conscious of the hollowness of appeals to Integrity as a separable entity in itself, alert to the complex process by which new vanities and new moral aspirations wake to life simultaneously within human beings. And *yet none of this knowledge paralyzes me.* I assess the relative significance of the character's conscience in my inward experience as I read; I understand that Oblonsky is a small man, less than a man can be, and in the act of understanding I rise for a while above the naïf or gull within me, above my smallness, and out of chichi self-contempt.

A voice says: It sounds mysterious. Reading and writing fiction equal judging yourself from outside, judging another from within. . . . Can you tell it simpler, please?

It's not, finally, a simple matter, I suppose. And for that reason people who talk about fiction in terms of volume of news, competition with Huntley-Brinkley, or with Mailer at a convention, or Capote at an execution, seem to me (I confess) dim. A story is an orchestration or score of sympathy and judgment, penetration and objectification: now the one predominates, now the other, but both are always at hand, stimulating each other, letting us out of ourselves, calling us back to judge our trip. I need such scores for several reasons. Partly because through them it's possible to touch a life of feeling or an idea of personhood superior to the one in current journalistic fashion, yet not so far beyond me as that still proposed by the religious establishments. Partly because the possession of a means of motion forth from the self spins me out of simplicities of self-laceration and doom-mongering. Partly because, through the novel—again: either by writing or reading it—I touch my borders, such as they are, become an expanded constructive sympathy, an expanded self. No more rewinding myself perpetually onto the spindle of a passive shame: I spring with the word toward its target and take the force of the impact from within.

—Fine, oh, fine, says a harsher voice: I get it. Writing fiction is

an ego rub. It builds self-satisfaction. It lets you like yourself.
—You think that's proper? In a time like this we should go about
savoring our beauties and excellences?

Well, it hurts to say so, true. And no use pointing out, defensively, that there are complacencies in stylized guilt (the news of
my whole life) as well as in shrugging self-acceptance. For, once
that point is made, you're back again in abstract argument,
speaking up solemnly for some famous elusive "balanced attitude
toward life," etc. Who can know what balance is? The best I
know is that I like truth of the sort implicit in Thoreau's lovely
springy sentence: "When I am condemned and condemn myself
utterly, I think straightway, 'But I rely on love for some things.' "
I like, that is to say, a truth of resiliency, a truth about how we
spring out, spring back, aren't by any means "indomitable," yet
seldom are put down by sorrow or guilt, can cross over, can know
from within. Such truth doesn't belong to the new journalism; the
mode is too uniformly blackish and self-accusatory. But in the
bright book of life, the novel, you can sometimes touch it—which
is why, even in a bad moment, people will get on with the work.

—Well and good, says one last voice, kinder and more relaxed.
But you've not said how it really went out there, have you? Out
in Hollywood? You remember you started—

How it *really* went? In the end that's another subject, not at all
close to the one in view here (is fiction finished?). It is the
subject of values shaken, the challenge of fantasy—not fit stuff
(to repeat) either for Involvedese or for the lingo of the Culture
Critic. The subject does come up, though, in something of mine
available for a price downtown—a book that has, for a stretch, a
Hollywood setting. The work is called A Novel, and I can speak
of it at any time without feeling pushy, guilty, or the like. For the
idea of speaking of it is only to rouse a pleasant memory. Thinking back on "the work," talking about it, I remember writing
it—the experience rushes into mind, the freedom, sense of per-
fectability. . . . How happy I was!—happiness being nothing
more nor less than a road by which it does seem possible truly to
get there from here.

Acknowledgments

The author thanks Theodore Baird, Fred Baron, Seelye Bixler, John Cameron, Muriel Crosson, Larry Dilg, Barbara Hardy, George Kateb, Leo Marx, Bea McKie, James Merrill, Floyd Merritt, Dave Michelmore, Lewis Mudge, Franklin Patterson, William Pritchard, Edwin Rozwenc, John Simon, James Steinman, and Rosa White for generous help of many kinds.

A leading critic, essayist and novelist, Benjamin DeMott is a Professor of English at Amherst College in Massachusetts, where he lives with his wife and four children.